Why Can't Mother Vote?

For Farrell Varner,
—Best regards!
— Bill Hal

High praise for *Why Can't Mother Vote?*

"For a century, Joe Hanover has remained a forgotten hero of American democracy, but now his inspiring story is revealed in William Haltom's *Why Can't Mother Vote?* As a young immigrant to Memphis who believed in the American dream of equality and opportunity for all, then as a young legislator willing to stand up for justice against fierce opposition, Hanover became a champion of women's suffrage. When the fight to ratify the Nineteenth Amendment came to Tennessee in 1920, Hanover rose to lead the suffragists' fight in the statehouse. Haltom helps us recognize Joe Hanover as a true patriot, and we need the lesson of his life more than ever."

–**Elaine Weiss**, author of *The Woman's Hour*

" 'To thine own self be true' is a timeless guiding principle, and Joe Hanover's energetic and courageous story is a wonderful example of what a difference integrity can make. Bill Haltom brings Joe Hanover to life in an educational and entertaining way that makes for enjoyable and inspiring reading!"

–**Tom Vickstrom**, hotel historian, The Hermitage Hotel, Nashville

"In *Why Can't Mother Vote?* Bill Haltom shares the path to success of the final ratification of the Suffrage Amendment through the efforts of Joseph Hanover. We learn of Hanover's journey from the pogroms of Poland to the opportunities of Memphis. Driven by his love for his mother and his veneration of America's founding documents, Hanover uses his skills as an attorney and lawmaker to shepherd woman suffrage through the convoluted machinations of the political process. In telling the story, Haltom gives Hanover his rightful place in history."

–**Dr. Janann Sherman**, co-author of *The Perfect 36: Tennessee Delivers Woman Suffrage* and retired University of Memphis history department chair

"Bill Haltom's story of one lawyer's drive for fairness and equality for women should make each of us stand taller as we go about the unfinished business of democracy."

–**Judy Perry Martinez**, president, American Bar Association

"One of the nation's leading male voices in the woman suffrage movement was Joe Hanover, a Polish immigrant, Memphian, lawyer, state representative, and ultimately the floor leader for the passage of the Nineteenth Amendment in the Tennessee House of Representatives. One of Tennessee's favorite contemporary storytellers, Bill Haltom, brilliantly chronicles Hanover's journey from childhood to ratification leader. Haltom's compelling writing humanizes Hanover and other major players in this true tale of intrigue, racial bias, big business, and moral conflict that dramatically forever changed the face of democracy in America."

—**Sarah Sheppeard**, president, Tennessee Bar Association

"This well-written and fascinating story of an unsung hero, *Why Can't Mother Vote?*, highlights the most unlikely figure in securing passage of the Nineteenth Amendment to the US Constitution. Bill Haltom has crafted an engaging and inspiring read about a Southern Jewish immigrant and Tennessee state representative named Joseph Hanover whose courageous leadership in 1920 helped make America a more perfect union."

—**Micah D. Greenstein**, senior rabbi, Temple Israel, Memphis

"This story about Joe Hanover is heartening and a must-read for anyone valuing democracy and the ability to cast a vote. Bill Haltom has woven a vivid, front-row-seat tale of this American who made an enormous difference in our country's future by steadfastly supporting suffrage in Tennessee, the last state needed to ratify the Nineteenth Amendment. With striking backdrops of the mighty Mississippi River, The Hermitage Hotel, and Tennessee's Capitol, Haltom describes the 'War of the Roses' and all the negotiating in the battle over whether or not a woman should be able to vote. Not glossing over the veiled elements of power and white supremacy that were also at play during the lead-up to the suffrage vote, Haltom chronicles the racism of the time, as well as Hanover's measured, level-headed responses. As an immigrant, a lawyer, a Memphian, and a legislator, Hanover was the hero who was needed at that moment. Without him and his efforts, we would not be celebrating the 100th anniversary of women's right to vote. And just try and get through the end of Chapter 14—the description of Hanover's mother going to cast her ballot for the first time—without a tear in your eye."

—**Suzanne Craig Robertson**, editor, *Tennessee Bar Journal*

"Bill Haltom writes with the clarity of a beautiful crystal and the straightforwardness of an arrow to the target. He tells the story of Joseph Hanover from a frozen lake in Poland, where as a child he was smuggled to freedom, to the Pinch and Binghampton districts of Memphis. Hanover believed deeply in the Declaration of Independence, the Constitution, freedom, and opportunity that came with American citizenship. Joseph became a lawyer and a businessman before being elected to the Tennessee General Assembly in 1918 and 1920. Haltom chronicles excerpts from Hanover's life and the suffragist movement climaxing at The Hermitage Hotel in Nashville in the 'War of Roses.' The 30-year-old legislator kept the movement in Tennessee alive with his haunting question, 'Why can't Mother vote?' Hanover's valiant efforts, legislative prowess, and gifted oratory resulted in Tennessee's vote as the thirty-sixth state to ratify the Nineteenth Amendment to the Constitution. Finally, Joseph Hanover could answer his profound question and his mother had the right to vote."

—**Dr. Shirley C. Raines**, first woman president of the University of Memphis; on many occasions, she can be seen donning a white dress with a yellow rose

Why Can't Mother Vote?

Joseph Hanover and the
Unfinished Business of Democracy

By Bill Haltom

Library of Congress Cataloging-in-Publication Data

ISBN: 978-1-7333626-3-4

Printed and bound in the United States of America by Ingram Lightning Source

First edition

Editing, layout, and design: Jacque Hillman and Katie Gould

Editing: Paula Casey

Cover illustration and design: Wanda Stanfill

The HillHelen Group LLC
127 Fairmont Ave.
Jackson, TN 38301
hillhelengroup@gmail.com

In loving memory of my mother, Margaret Barron Haltom.
A lifelong Republican, she voted every election day if for no other
reason than to counter the vote of my father, a lifelong Democrat.

"The right of citizens of the United States to vote shall not be denied
or abridged by the United States or by any State on account of sex."
—*The Nineteenth Amendment of the United States Constitution*

"Ours is the great Volunteer State, and women from east, west,
north, and south are looking to us to give them political freedom.
The entire world has cast its eyes on Tennessee. This is a moral
question, and that's why I am here voting for this amendment . . .
that ours may truly be a democracy."
—*Rep. Joseph Hanover on the floor
of the Tennessee House of Representatives, August 17, 1920*

Acknowledgments

One of the joys of writing a biography is that you get to know a fascinating person. Sometimes you meet them personally in interviews and conversations. On other occasions, when the subject of your writing passed away long ago, you "meet" him or her by reviewing writings by and about them and, if given the opportunity, by talking with family, friends, and colleagues who knew them well.

My dear friends Paula Casey and Jocelyn Wurzburg, two twenty-first century suffragists, introduced me to Joe Hanover when they suggested that I research and write his remarkable story.

I got to know Joe Hanover by spending time with people who knew him well. As usual, it started with family, as I interviewed Joe's grandnephews Brad Hanover, Eddie Kaplan, Jerry Schwartz, and Steve Schwartz, and his grandniece Phyllis Levine. They told me great stories about "Uncle Joe" and shared family scrapbooks, correspondence, news clippings, and photos.

Jimmy Jalenak practiced law with "Mr. Joe" for several years and shared stories about the law firm that Joe, his brother David, his nephew "Skip," the late Billy Walsh, and Jalenak himself built and enjoyed over the years.

Micah Greenstein of Temple Israel and archivist Jennifer Kollath opened up the synagogue's library for me, containing a treasure trove of documents, magazines, newspaper articles, and photos of and about the Hanover family.

Jean Roseman, the author of *Shalom Nashville*, provided wonderful information about the role the Jewish women of Nashville played in the fight for woman suffrage.

Ronald Lee of the Tennessee State Library, Shelby County election commissioner Robert Meyers, and associate commissioner Carol Collinsworth helped me find information on the election of the independent Joe Hanover to the Tennessee General Assembly in 1918 and his re-election in 1920 after the governor declared his seat vacated.

The great Robert Caro has written that a biography should contain "a sense of place," an understanding and description of the setting of the life of the biography's subject. For Joe, that place in the summer of 1920 was The Hermitage Hotel in Nashville. Tom Vickstrom, historian of the iconic hotel, helped me understand the sense of place in the hotel's majestic lobby, anterooms, and suites in August 1920.

But the folks who best helped me get to know and admire Joe were and are writers who began to tell his story long before I met him. At the top of this list is the late Carol Lynn Yellin. Her classic article, "Countdown in Tennessee, 1920," was published in *American Heritage* in December 1978, and first told the story of how the Volunteer State became the "Perfect 36." This led to her book, *The Perfect 36: Tennessee Delivers Woman Suffrage*, co-authored with Dr. Janann Sherman, published in 1998.

If Carol Lynn Yellin were still with us, she would have been the perfect author for this book. I am indebted to her and to Dr. Janann Sherman for enabling me to build on their writing by focusing on Joe's role in helping make Tennessee the Perfect 36.

My friendship with Joe was also inspired and informed by the writing of Elaine Weiss, the author of the quintessential work on the battle for women's right to vote, *The Woman's Hour*. As set forth in the bibliography, it was a major source for my getting to know Joe.

It is one thing to tell a story, but we storytellers have to find the right words and get them on paper. I could not have done this without the help of my wonderful personal assistant, Sandy White, and my remarkably talented editor, Jacque Hillman.

I embarked on my journey with Joe Hanover with the encouragement and support of a number of fellow writers, including Amanda Swanson, Inman Majors, Robert Hicks, Keel Hunt, Dan Conaway, Sam Elliott, Suzanne Robertson, Roy Herron, Dawn LaFon, Neil White, Nick McCall, Scot Danforth, Jason Long, and Sally and John Thomason.

My dear friends Pam Reeves, Charles Swanson, Chris Vescovo, Sarah Sheppeard, Ben Alford, Charles Huddleston, Judy Johnson, Loretta Harber, Sharon Lee, Barbara Mayden, Allan Ramsaur, John Ryder, Buck Lewis, Jane Van Deren, and Lucian Pera have supported me in my writing efforts over many years.

And my love for telling stories has long been shared at breakfast with my

Baguette Brothers and at lunch with my Little Tea Shop colleagues Suhair Lauck, Charlie Newman, John Malmo, Ken Neill, and John Vergos.

I am also grateful to my former partners and colleagues at the Lewis Thomason law firm for supporting me during the forty years I was a full-time lawyer and part-time writer, although I am sure at times they thought it was the other way around!

Finally, like Joe, I am blessed to have a great family. My children—Will, Ken, and Margaret Grace—grew up hearing Daddy tell them stories about inspirational people, and they have encouraged me to continue to do it.

Above all, I am indebted to their mother, the love of my life, Claudia Swafford Haltom. She knows that I am neither a scholar nor a journalist, but she does believe I can tell a great story.

I hope you agree.

Table of Contents

Prologue: The Lobby of The Hermitage Hotel, August 18, 1920   1

1. A Frozen Lake in Poland   9

2. A New Life . . . in Memphis and Binghampton   15

3. Why Can't Mother Vote?   21

4. A Calling to Law   25

5. The Election of an Independent   31

6. The Fight for Partial Suffrage   37

7. Removal and Re-election   45

8. A Summons from Mrs. Catt   53

9. The Battle of the Women of Faith   61

10. "You're a Pretty Cheap Vote—They Are Paying Others a Thousand!"   67

11. "A White Man's Country!"   75

12. "The Hour Has Come!"   81

13. False Affidavits and the Red Rose Brigade Heads for Alabama   89

14. Signed, Sealed, and Delivered   95

15. Election Day 1920 . . . and Beyond   101

Epilogue: Joe Hanover Returns to Memphis   109

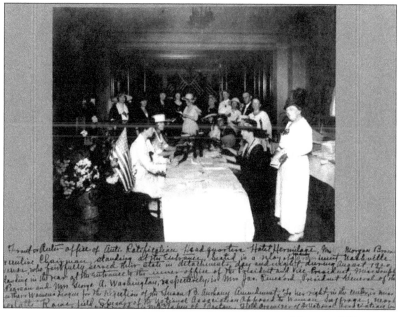

On August 18, 1920, Tennessee became the thirty-sixth state to ratify the Nineteenth Amendment, granting all American women the right to vote. The Hermitage Hotel, serving as the headquarters for suffragists and anti-suffragists, was a central location for this time in history.

Prologue:
The Lobby of The
Hermitage Hotel,
August 18, 1920

Photo courtesy of The Hermitage Hotel Archives

Known as Nashville's first million-dollar hotel, The Hermitage Hotel's grand opening was September 17, 1910. Guest rooms were paneled in mahogany and offered running ice water, a telephone, and a private bath. If only its walls could talk about the many conversations held in the pro-suffrage and anti-suffrage suites in 1920. The eighth floor was dedicated to sample rooms for traveling salesmen to exhibit their goods. It was on this floor that many legislators gathered to savor Jack Daniel's whiskey in August 1920.

Thirty-year-old state Rep. Joseph Hanover walked through the grand lobby of the elegant hotel to be greeted by deafening cheers and jeers.

The cheers came from a multitude of women in white dresses adorned with yellow roses, the symbol of their support for the proposed Nineteenth Amendment to the United States Constitution, granting women the right to vote. The jeers came from scores of other women, also wearing roses, but their roses were red, the symbol of their opposition to woman suffrage.

There were men in the crowd as well, some donning yellow rose boutonnieres on their seersucker suits, others wearing red. And there were a few politicians in the crowd with both yellow and red roses pinned to their lapels, as they tried to straddle the floral fence.

The national media called it the "War of the Roses."

Walking alongside Representative Hanover was a tall, handsome Nashville police officer, Capt. Paul Bush. Tennessee Gov. A. H. Roberts had assigned

Captain Bush to be Joe Hanover's bodyguard, and young Hanover needed him. In recent days, there had been numerous threats on Hanover's life. On one occasion, Hanover had been physically assaulted in the hotel elevator, his assailant calling him a "Bolshevik" and a "kike."

Both the adoration and the hatred of Hanover had emerged for the same reason. Hanover had become the nation's leading male voice in the fight for woman suffrage.

For more than seventy years, American women had fought for the most important right of any citizen of the United States: the right to vote. The founding fathers had granted the right in the Constitution, but for the first 131 years of the republic, voting had been the exclusive right of men, and, for the most part, white men.

But beginning with a meeting in Seneca Falls, New York, in 1848, generations of women had petitioned, marched, and vigorously lobbied for the political emancipation of half the nation, only to be scorned, humiliated, and, in some cases, even imprisoned.

With the passage of the Fourteenth Amendment in 1868 guaranteeing all citizens "the equal protection of the law," many thought the campaign for woman suffrage had been won. But in 1875, the United States Supreme Court unanimously ruled in the case of *Minor v. Happersett* that the Fourteenth Amendment did not grant women the right to vote.

In 1878, Sen. Aaron Seacrest of California introduced in the United States Senate the Anthony Amendment, named in honor of the great suffragist Susan B. Anthony, seeking a constitutional amendment guaranteeing women their right to vote. The proposed amendment languished in a Senate committee for nine years until the Senate rejected it in 1887 by a vote of 16–34.

The battle for woman suffrage continued for the next three decades, with some incremental gains as a few states passed legislation enacting either full or partial suffrage for women.

In 1914, a constitutional amendment to grant women the right to vote was proposed again in the US Senate, but it was rejected again.

But the movement for woman suffrage gained momentum in 1918 when President Woodrow Wilson spoke in favor of it in his State of the Union address.

A proposed Nineteenth Amendment was introduced again in Congress, and on October 1, 1918, President Wilson addressed the US Senate urging passage. He told the Senate, "I regard the extension of suffrage to women as vitally essential to the successful prosecution of the great war of humanity in which we are engaged." Despite the president's plea, the amendment proposal failed in the Senate by two votes.

Then on May 21, 1919, with yet another proposed Nineteenth Amendment before them, the US House of Representatives passed a resolution approving the Anthony Amendment by a vote of 342–89. Two weeks later, on June 4, 1919, the Senate finally passed the proposed amendment by a vote of 56–20.

At long last, a constitutional amendment for woman suffrage was being sent to the states for ratification. Thirty-six of the then-forty-eight states had to ratify the proposed amendment for it to become the law of the land.

Initially, support for ratification lined up quickly, with five states passing ratification within a week after the amendment was submitted by Congress. Nine more states joined in support for ratification in the summer and fall of 1919. By March of the following year, thirty-five states had approved the proposed amendment. One more state was needed to grant American women the constitutional right to vote.

And then the process bogged down. Seven Southern states rejected the amendment. There was even talk in Ohio, which had been one of the first states to pass ratification, of reconvening the legislature to reconsider the matter.

By the summer of 1920, the battle for the passage of the Nineteenth Amendment had come down to one state–Tennessee.

On August 7, 1920, Governor Roberts issued a proclamation calling the 61st Tennessee General Assembly into an extraordinary session at the State Capitol on the following Monday to debate and vote on ratification of the amendment.

On Sunday, August 8, Hanover had taken the train from his hometown of Memphis, made the 220-mile trip to Nashville's Union Station, and checked into The Hermitage Hotel.

The hotel was packed not only with legislators, but also with suffragists ("the Suffs"), anti-suffragists ("the Antis"), lobbyists, reporters, bootleggers, and preachers.

Carrie Chapman Catt, president of the National American Woman Suffrage Association, with two million members nationwide, was in a suite on the third floor, a command post in the effort to secure the legislators' passage of the Nineteenth Amendment.

In rooms alongside the hotel's mezzanine, Josephine Anderson Pearson of Monteagle, Tennessee, president of the Tennessee Association Opposed to Woman Suffrage, marshaled the resistance.

US Sen. Kenneth D. McKellar had come from Washington to lobby for passage of the amendment with the support of President Woodrow Wilson.

Charl Ormond Williams, vice chairman of the Democratic National Committee, had come from Memphis to lend her administrative skills to the Suffs at the request of Governor Roberts.

The venerable lobby of The Hermitage Hotel had become known as "the third house of the Tennessee legislature," along with the Tennessee Senate and House of Representatives. Its Italian marble floors, soaring archways, and vaulted ceiling had become the eye of the storm in Tennessee's "War of the Roses."

Initially, it appeared the extraordinary session would be a short one. The state Senate quickly passed the resolution of ratification by a vote of 25–4 after only three hours of debate.

Passage in the House also seemed a foregone conclusion as sixty-two of the ninety-nine members had executed written pledges of support for ratification as the session began.

But the most powerful member of the Tennessee House of Representatives, Speaker Seth Walker of Lebanon, reversed his position and became a fiery opponent of the amendment. Playing the race card, Walker declared that America was a "white man's country," warning that the passage of the amendment would guarantee the right to vote not only to women but to blacks as well.

The powerful Louisville and Nashville Railroad sent its lobbyists to The Hermitage Hotel to urge legislators to vote against the amendment.

Even Jack Daniel's joined the opposition. Despite the recently passed Eighteenth Amendment to the Constitution ushering in Prohibition, the liquor industry flourished or, more accurately, flowed in Tennessee, and its leaders were opposed to woman suffrage. They opened what became known as the "Jack Daniel's Suite" on the eighth floor of the hotel where they plied legislators with bourbon in an effort to win their hearts, minds, and throats.

Jack Daniel's formed an unholy alliance with evangelical preachers across the state as well as with the Women's Christian Temperance Union. The preachers and their sober sisters held anti-suffrage rallies at the Ryman Auditorium and in local churches across the state.

The sixty-two pledges fell to fifty-five and then down to forty-seven. With the final debate and vote on the horizon, Catt called Hanover into her suite. She asked him to lead the legislative fight for the passage of ratification.

Catt's selection of Hanover as the leader was a curious one. Even Hanover did not understand it. He was a freshman legislator who had been elected as an independent. He had no political power to wield in terms of patronage, influence, or money. He was a "city boy" in an overwhelmingly rural legislature, and he was one of only two Jews in the General Assembly, a body dominated by evangelical Christians.

The most powerful forces in Tennessee politics—including the speaker of the House, the L&N Railroad, Jack Daniel's, and the preachers—opposed Hanover. But he was not going to back away from the fight. Because of his own unique background, he believed deeply in the Constitution of the United States and the Bill of Rights, and he wanted the rights granted therein to be afforded to every American.

As Hanover exited the hotel lobby that morning and headed up Sixth Avenue two blocks to the Capitol, he embarked on the longest day of his young life. Before the day was over, he would face false claims of bribery, slander, and even kidnapping. At the end of the day, a seventy-two-year battle for woman suffrage would come to a conclusion.

For Joe Hanover, the day would also mark the end of a long personal journey . . . a journey that had begun some twenty-five years earlier on a frozen lake in Poland.

In the lobby of The Hermitage Hotel, a colorful crowd gathered, consisting of pro-suffrage leaders wearing yellow roses and anti-suffrage leaders wearing red roses. They walked on Tennessee marble lobby floors and stood near Italian marble columns. Above them soared the magnificent painted glass skylight, still seen today.

A Frozen Lake
in Poland

A young Joe Hanover (center) poses with his family.

Wolfe and Esther Hanover are pictured here with their sons Ben and Morris. Joe Hanover is in the center.

I t was one of Joseph Hanover's earliest memories, but there were no images in that memory, only darkness and bitter cold.

It was midwinter 1895, and six-year-old Joe was tucked into a gunnysack on the back of a man he did not know. The stranger was secretly toting Joe across a lake in eastern Poland. Close behind them were Joe's mother, Esther, and his older brothers, Benjamin and Morris.

The Hanovers were taking their first steps on a precarious journey from their home in Pultusk, Poland, to a new home thousands of miles away in the United States of America.

Joe's father, Wolfe Hanover, had made the trip two years earlier after the czar of Russia confiscated the Hanover family's land and possessions. Wolfe Hanover was determined to help his family flee the pogroms, the persecution and oppression of Jews in eastern Poland. He made his way to the United States and wrote his family that they would soon be reunited in "the land of freedom, equality, and justice."

Wolfe Hanover found his way first to New York City, where he worked briefly as a cobbler. He moved to St. Louis, finding other job opportunities and a chance to earn money to finance his family's exodus to America. After a short time there, he made his way south down the Mississippi River to Memphis, where his cousin Morris had lived for a number of years after his own escape from Poland.

Upon arriving in Memphis virtually penniless, Wolfe found housing in the Pinch neighborhood, home to many Orthodox Jewish immigrants, most of them from Poland like the Hanovers. Wolfe first worked as a peddler, selling merchandise he obtained on credit from his cousin Morris and other settled immigrants. After a few months of peddling, he was able to open his own dry goods store in the Pinch on Main Street.

As Wolfe made money, he sent almost all of it back to his family in Poland. By 1895, he had forwarded Esther and his sons sufficient funds to purchase second-class tickets aboard a Holland Line steamship for the trip to America, plus $500 to pay a "bootlegger" to guide the family out of Poland.

It was the bootlegger who was carrying young Joe in his gunnysack across the frozen lake.

As she walked closely behind the bootlegger and her then-youngest child, Esther Hanover gripped the hands of Joe's brothers. In the wig atop her head, Esther hid the precious funds for the trip. In her stocking was a large salami she would use to feed her sons.

The bootlegger earned his pay, getting Joe, his mother, and his brothers safely across the Polish border to docks along the Baltic Sea. There the Hanovers boarded the steamship for the trip to America.

Like the journey across the frozen lake, the cruise across the Atlantic was treacherous. Joe, his mother, and his brothers were ensconced in the bottom of the steamship. The ship's captain generously sent food down to the family, but Joe's mother never took a bite. She was seasick for the entire voyage.

But six-year-old Joe did have one memorable and wonderful experience aboard the steamship. One evening while his mother and brothers tried to sleep, Joe found his way up to the first-class deck where a big orchestra was entertaining the affluent passengers. Joe made his way to the center of the dance floor in front of the big band and proceeded to tap dance. The crowd loved him. They cheered and tossed him money, which Joe happily collected in his cap.

The money Joe earned dancing that evening came in handy to Esther after she and her sons made it to New York City, through Ellis Island, and boarded a train for another trip, this time a joyful one. They were headed to Memphis, where Wolfe Hanover would welcome them to their new home.

Photo courtesy of the Hanover family

Wolfe Hanover constantly reminded his sons how blessed they were to be living in the United States of America.

2

A New Life . . . in Memphis and Binghampton

BROAD ST LOOKING SOUTH.   BINGHAMPTON TENN.

After living in the Pinch for several years, the Hanovers moved to Binghampton, another vibrant immigrant community five miles east of downtown Memphis. There Wolfe Hanover opened W. C. Hanover & Sons, a dry goods store on Broad, seen here circa 1911.

I n the closing years of the nineteenth century, the Hanovers were not the only family of immigrants seeking a new life in Memphis. There were thousands of such immigrants in the city, many of whom, like the Hanovers, had fled Eastern Europe to escape the czar, pogroms, and persecution.

Memphis was a fitting place for immigrants to seek a new life inasmuch as the city itself was rebuilding its civic life after trials and tribulations.

The city on a bluff overlooking the Mississippi River had been founded in 1819 by Andrew Jackson, John Overton, and James Winchester. In the ensuing decades, Memphis became a major river port and was growing into the largest spot cotton market in the world, as well as a major trading center for lumber. But in the 1870s, a yellow fever epidemic decimated the city. Panic ensued. More than 25,000 Memphians fled the city, many never to return. Of the 19,000 citizens who remained, 17,000 contracted the fever and more than 5,000 died. The city went bankrupt and surrendered its charter.

But the city charter was restored in 1893, the economy boomed, and by 1900 the city's population had grown to more than 100,000, with many of those citizens immigrants like the Hanovers.

The Hanovers' first home in Memphis was in the Pinch, a twelve-block area north of downtown. The Pinch offered a network of support for immigrants, including a synagogue and businesses. There were also kosher markets and several delis.

Like many new residents of the Pinch, Wolfe Hanover was soon able to open his own dry goods store at 90 Main Street, and when six-year-old Joe, his mother, and his brothers arrived in Memphis, the store became their first home in America, as they lived upstairs above the merchandise floor.

The Hanovers worshiped at Anshei Sphard, a synagogue founded by Orthodox Jewish immigrants from Poland.

The Pinch also had a Jewish Neighborhood House, a community center that provided classes in English and other programs to help immigrants adjust to life in the United States of America.

Above all, the Pinch had a spirit of enterprise that no doubt affirmed Wolfe Hanover's belief that he had found his family a new home in a land of freedom and opportunity.

After living in the Pinch for a couple of years, the Hanovers moved to a new home in Binghampton, another vibrant immigrant community just five miles east of downtown Memphis. There, Wolfe opened W. C. Hanover & Sons, a dry goods store on Broad Avenue where, true to its name, Joe, Ben, and Morris Hanover joined their father in the operation of the business. In time, there would be two other sons working in W. C. Hanover & Sons: David and Sam, both born in America.

Joe Hanover loved Binghampton. He particularly enjoyed visiting the nearby Memphis Fairgrounds, which featured a horseracing track. Joe loved watching the thoroughbreds race, and he dreamed that someday he would raise horses of his own that would race in Memphis and perhaps beyond.

Joe was living in an extraordinary new land of freedom, business opportunities, and even horses, and no czar was going to take that away from him. Joe did not take any of this for granted. He was deeply grateful and would be patriotic about his new country for the rest of his life.

Joe, Ben, and Morris Hanover joined their father, Wolfe, in W. C. Hanover & Sons. In time, David and Sam, both born in America, would work in the store.

Wolfe Hanover often told his sons they had come to the land of freedom and opportunity.

Esther Hanover and her husband, Wolfe, studied the Declaration of Independence and the Constitution of the United States when they became naturalized citizens of the United States. Esther encouraged her sons to do so as well, and Joe studied at night by oil lamp.

3

Why Can't
Mother Vote?

Photo courtesy of Mia Pacht

Esther worked hard rearing her five boys and taking care of her family. In this photo, she holds her granddaughter, Mia Pacht. As he grew older, Joe Hanover realized that despite the freedoms promised in America, a precious right afforded by the Constitution was not available to his mother.

hy can't Mother vote? It was a question young Joe Hanover asked his parents on several occasions. They never had an answer.

Wolfe Hanover constantly reminded his sons how blessed they were to be living in the United States of America. He would remind them of this blessing as he thanked God for helping the Hanovers escape the oppression of the czar and the persecution of Jews in Eastern Europe. He would tell his sons on an almost daily basis how thankful they should be for their new country as they worked together in the dry goods store on Broad Avenue.

Joe's mother, Esther, also wanted Joe and his brothers to appreciate their new country. But she wanted something more. She wanted them to understand their new homeland and the principles and values for which America supposedly stood.

Both Esther and Wolfe Hanover had become naturalized American citizens. They had been sworn in as new Americans before the Shelby County Criminal Court, as they had to execute documents disavowing any allegiance to the czar of Russia. They had to make such pledges inasmuch as their previous homeland, Poland, was under the control of Russia.

Wolfe and Esther Hanover had no problem whatsoever signing such documents. They had come to America to escape such a tyrant, and Wolfe would often say proudly that there were "no tyrants in America." Joe would remember that line and refer to it often during the course of his life.

In becoming new citizens, Wolfe and Esther had read the Declaration of Independence and the Constitution of the United States. Esther encouraged her sons to do so as well.

Joe did what he was told. He would read the American documents by an oil lamp at night, and he was impressed by the rule of law that governed America and the rights that were to be granted to every American citizen.

But as Joe studied these documents, he began to wonder why the privileges set forth in the Bill of Rights were not available, in reality, to all citizens. Binghampton was a racially integrated community, but it was a part of the Jim Crow South. The Constitution that young Joe read said in the Fourteenth Amendment that all citizens were afforded "the equal protection of the laws." Young Joe recognized that did not apply to the black residents of Binghampton.

And in an issue literally close to home, Joe realized that perhaps the most precious right afforded by the Constitution was not available to his mother, even though she had become a naturalized citizen of the United States of America.

His mother was not allowed to vote.

"Why can't Mother vote?" Joe asked his parents.

Wolfe and Esther simply replied that the right was not afforded to her.

Young Joe believed deeply in the American dream, a dream that was coming true for him, having crossed that frozen lake in Poland.

But he also began to understand that the nation he now called home was a work in progress. The rights set forth in the United States Constitution were not being offered to each and every citizen, including his own mother.

Simply put, there was unfinished business in America.

Joe did not realize it at the time, but in a few years, he was going to help America take care of some of that unfinished business.

A Calling to Law

IN CONGRESS, JULY 4, 1776.

A DECLARATION

BY THE REPRESENTATIVES OF THE

UNITED STATES OF AMERICA,

IN GENERAL CONGRESS ASSEMBLED.

WHEN in the Course of human Events, it becomes necessary for one People to dissolve the Political Bands which have connected them with another, and to assume among the Powers of the Earth, the separate and equal Station to which the Laws of Nature and of Nature's God entitle them, a decent Respect to the Opinions of Mankind requires that they should declare the causes which impel them to the Separation.

We hold these Truths to be self-evident, that all Men are created equal, that they are endowed by their Creator with certain unalienable Rights, that among these are Life, Liberty, and the Pursuit of Happiness—That to secure these Rights, Governments are instituted among Men, deriving their just Powers from the Consent of the Governed, that whenever any Form of Government becomes destructive of these Ends, it is the Right of the People to alter or to abolish it, and to institute new Government, laying its Foundation on such Principles, and organizing its Powers in such Form, as to them shall seem most likely to effect their Safety and Happiness. Prudence, indeed, will dictate that Governments long established should not be changed for light and transient Causes; and accordingly all Experience hath shewn, that Mankind are more disposed to suffer, while Evils are sufferable, than to right themselves by abolishing the Forms to which they are accustomed. But when a long Train of Abuses and Usurpations, pursuing invariably the same Object, evinces a Design to reduce them under absolute Despotism, it is their Right, it is their Duty, to throw off such Government, and to provide new Guards for their future Security. Such has been the patient Sufferance of these Colonies; and such is now the Necessity which constrains them to alter their former Systems of Government. The History of the present King of Great-Britain is a History of repeated Injuries and Usurpations, all having in direct Object the Establishment of an absolute Tyranny over these States. To prove this, let Facts be submitted to a candid World.

At the turn of the twentieth century, young Joe Hanover was enrolled in the Market Street School in downtown Memphis, a few blocks from his first home in the Pinch. The school was on the bluff, just a block from the banks of the Mississippi River. Before and after classes, Joe and his schoolmates would sit on the levee and watch the scene on the majestic river below them. Joe admired the steamboats, their decks piled high with cotton, that would dock at the city's cobblestone waterfront. He watched the cotton being loaded onto carts that mules pulled up the levee.

The river and the commerce he witnessed moving upon it inspired Joe. The river seemed to exemplify his new homeland. Like the thoroughbreds he loved to watch run at the Memphis Fairgrounds, the steamships and barges he saw on the river made Joe dream of where he himself would be headed in the coming years in his new land.

It was the beginning of a lifelong love for the Mississippi River, as he would someday chair the Memphis and Shelby County Port Commission.

Joe also loved the Market Street School. It gave him the opportunity to learn more about his new country, as he followed up on his reading of the Declaration of Independence and the US Constitution at home.

Market Street School was Memphis's first high school, and Joe hoped to complete twelve years of formal education there. But in the early years of the twentieth century, working-class kids like Joe could not afford the luxury of even a free public education. They were expected to begin working as soon as they were able.

After the eighth grade, Joe left the Market Street School to work full time in two jobs: working by day at W. C. Hanover & Sons in Binghampton and at night at Benjamin's Saloon, a Binghampton bar and nightclub operated by his brother.

But in 1911, Joe resumed his formal education, albeit on a part-time basis. He enrolled in the Southern Law School, a night law school in downtown Memphis located close to the Market Street School.

The Southern Law School was not connected with any college or university. It did not have a faculty comprised of academic professors. Its teachers were Memphis lawyers and judges.

Affluent young Memphis men of that time who wanted to be lawyers would leave the city to attend law school at the University of Virginia, Vanderbilt University, the University of Tennessee, or the University of Mississippi. But Joe and his fellow Southern Law School students worked one or more jobs during the day, attended class at night, and then returned to their homes to study law by the light of oil lamps.

While the Southern Law School did not have the prestige of the University of Virginia or Vanderbilt Law School, it offered Joe wonderful training on what lawyers do and how they do it. There was nothing abstract about legal education at the Southern Law School. It was nuts and bolts, and it prepared Joe for his future life in the law.

In 1914, Joe graduated from the Southern Law School and passed the Tennessee Bar. He immediately landed his first job in the legal profession—city attorney for Binghampton.

It was the beginning of a fabulous law career that would span seventy years. Joe's younger brother David, whom he had helped put through the Southern

Law School, soon joined him in his law practice. Joe and David would build one of the most powerful law firms in the state with accomplishments in courtrooms, political arenas, and, for Joe, at the racetracks.

In 1918, in just the fourth year of his budding young career, Joe decided he wanted to be more than a lawyer. He wanted to be a lawmaker. He decided to pursue a seat in the Tennessee House of Representatives, where he would be destined to help America take care of some unfinished business.

Edward Hull Crump, known as 'Boss Crump,' served three terms as mayor of Memphis from 1910 through 1915, but he effectively appointed every mayor for the next forty years. He also controlled most of the statewide elections in Tennessee. Joe Hanover considered Boss Crump a tyrant and compared him to the czar of Russia.

5

The Election
of an Independent

I n 1918, Memphis elections were under the firm control of one man—Edward Hull Crump. Appropriately called Boss Crump, he was first elected mayor of Memphis in 1909. His election not only marked the beginning of his tenure as "Boss" but was also part of the birth of the blues. W. C. Handy wrote Boss Crump's campaign theme song, "Mr. Crump's Blues," premiering it at Peewee's Saloon on Beale Street. The song was later renamed "Memphis Blues" and was Handy's first musical composition.

After serving three terms as mayor from 1910 to 1915, Boss Crump did not seek re-election. However, he effectively appointed every mayor of Memphis for the next forty years.

Boss Crump controlled not only Memphis elections but also most of the statewide elections in Tennessee for the first half of the twentieth century. Governors, congressmen, and senators were all elected with his blessings, and his opponents were invariably defeated.

He did not brook dissent. He demanded loyalty from those he put in office, and if you did not support his agenda, you would be defeated for re-election by a Crump-selected opponent.

Joe Hanover did not like Boss Crump. He regarded him as a tyrant, even comparing him to the czar of Russia, remembering his father's pronouncement that there were no tyrants in America, or at least there shouldn't be.

"My parents fled from an oppressive government (in Poland) and came here. They came to America for freedom from such oppressors," Hanover observed.

The young man who had studied the Declaration of Independence, the Constitution of the United States, and particularly the Bill of Rights felt that Boss Crump was the antithesis of what America should be about.

Hanover vigorously exercised his First Amendment right of free speech. When it came to Boss Crump, Hanover did not give himself, in the words of a later Tennessee politician, "the luxury of an unexpressed thought." He said clearly and unequivocally how he felt about the Boss.

When Hanover announced in early 1918 that he would be a candidate for the Tennessee House of Representatives, few people gave him a chance. Not only was he a recognized critic of Boss Crump, but he decided to run as an independent, eschewing the support of the Democratic Party. And in Memphis and Shelby County in 1918, there was really no two-party system. To win an election, you had to be a Democrat and, for that matter, a Democrat supported by Boss Crump.

Defying all odds, the Polish immigrant, now an American citizen, filed to run for the Tennessee legislature as an independent.

Boss Crump probably didn't spend too much time worrying about the young independent candidate from Binghampton. If he thought about it at all, he no doubt believed that the race for the election of the representative from Shelby County District No. 5 was a foregone conclusion.

But there were two facts about the Shelby District No. 5 race that made it unique. First was the electorate. Second was the independent candidate who sought to represent them.

The heart of Shelby District No. 5 was Hanover's adopted hometown, Binghampton. It was the home of many Joe Hanovers, immigrants who had come to America fleeing oppression. The voters knew Joe Hanover was one of them.

The other unique feature of this race was the independent candidate himself. Hanover had the natural ability of all good lawyers. He was a great storyteller.

He was also a fiery and patriotic orator. In his campaign speeches, he would tell voters the story of his own journey to America, across the frozen lake in Poland. He would talk about his study of the Declaration of Independence, the Constitution, and the Bill of Rights, and he would explain that he did not take democracy for granted and wished to go to the Tennessee legislature to support the principles of the country he loved.

On Election Day, November 5, 1918, Hanover surprised Boss Crump, winning the election by a comfortable margin. He later admitted the results even surprised him. The voters were sending him to Nashville to be a member of the 61st General Assembly. He was destined to be in a historic session in 1920.

Gov. A. H. Roberts signed the partial suffrage bill on the
last day of the legislative session, convinced that it would be
declared unconstitutional by the Tennessee Supreme Court.

6

The Fight
for Partial Suffrage

House Bill No. 717

"An act granting women the right to vote for electors of President and Vice President of the United States, and for municipal officers; to participate and vote in certain matters in elections; and prescribing the qualifications and conditions upon which women may exercise such right of suffrage."

hen Joseph Hanover was sworn in as a member of the Tennessee House of Representatives in early 1919, he was different from his ninety-eight colleagues in many respects.

First, he was an immigrant. Since no member of the General Assembly was a Native American, all of his colleagues were, in effect, immigrants. But Hanover was the only first-generation immigrant.

Second, he was an independent. Almost all of his colleagues from West and Middle Tennessee were Democrats. The few Republicans in the legislature at the time were from East Tennessee, the grand division of the state that had remained true to Lincoln and the Union during the Civil War.

Third, he was one of only two Jews in the legislature.

He was also a city boy in a legislature that was not just overwhelmingly rural. It was described by one Tennessee journalist as a "rollicking rural fiefdom."

But Hanover, the independent from Memphis, quickly won the respect and admiration of his colleagues.

First, the word quickly got around the Capitol that if anyone wanted a proposed bill written and wanted it done right, they should go see that city lawyer, Joe Hanover. He was willing to assist any and all of his colleagues in drafting legislation. Since he was independent, he provided legal assistance to both Democrats and Republicans, and he enjoyed doing it.

Second, the fact that he was an independent gained him bipartisan respect. He was not advancing the interest of one side versus the other. He was truly bipartisan in his willingness to work with his colleagues.

Hanover also won the respect and admiration of his colleagues because he was deeply patriotic. In his first speech on the floor of the legislature, he told his story—the story of how his father had helped him, his mother, and his brothers escape oppression in Eastern Europe. He told the story of how in America they had found a land of freedom and opportunity, as evidenced by the fact that this boy from Pultusk, Poland, was now a member of the Tennessee General Assembly.

A few weeks after joining the Tennessee legislature, he offered his support for House Bill No. 717, which stated:

"An act granting women the right to vote for electors of President and Vice President of the United States, and for municipal officers; to participate and vote in certain matters in elections; and prescribing the qualifications and conditions upon which women may exercise such right of suffrage."

The bill was a proposal for partial suffrage and was part of a strategy that had been developed by Carrie Chapman Catt, the president of the National American Woman Suffrage Association, to lead to the ultimate passage of a federal constitutional amendment that would grant all women in America the right to vote in all elections. The rationale of the "Winning Plan" was that with states granting some form of suffrage to women, it was more likely that federal legislators would support the passage of the proposed constitutional amendment.

It was also believed that legislators who resisted supporting a federal suffrage amendment could more easily accept partial suffrage. In effect, it would be the first step to achieving the long-overdue right to vote for women.

Hanover remembered asking his parents, "Why can't Mother vote?" Now he was making the initial move in seeing that she could.

Hanover joined his friends in the legislature in full support of the partial suffrage bill.

The proposal for partial suffrage quickly passed in the state Senate. It then came down to a vote of the Tennessee House of Representatives.

On April 14, 1919, freshman Rep. Joe Hanover spoke eloquently in favor of the passage of the partial suffrage bill. Again, his speech was deeply patriotic, as he expressed his love for his country and his belief that the treasured right to vote should be afforded to all citizens.

To his surprise that day, he was joined in support for ratification of partial suffrage by an unlikely ally—Seth Walker, the speaker of the Tennessee House of Representatives. Speaker Walker was the most powerful member of the Tennessee House, and he had previously expressed his strong opposition to woman suffrage. But after Hanover's speech in favor of partial suffrage, the speaker came down from his chair at the House rostrum, walked to the floor of the chamber, and, to the surprise of everyone present, announced that he had reconsidered his position and was now in favor of woman suffrage.

Speaker Walker reminded his fellow legislators that the right to vote had been granted to Negroes, and he argued it should also be extended to women.

"I declare to you that this is not right," he stated, "and that they (women) should have a voice in our government." He said it would be a "crime and a shame if women were not given this right."

With the support of the speaker of the House, the women's partial suffrage bill narrowly passed.

Partial suffrage for Tennessee women was not ideal. The final version of the bill that passed gave women, in effect, separate but equal enfranchisement, as women would be allowed to cast votes only in separate ballots from the men, and only in presidential and municipal elections. But it was the first step toward full suffrage for Tennessee women.

Tennessee Gov. A. H. Roberts was skeptical about the enactment of partial suffrage, as he was unsure of its impact on his own political future. He reluctantly signed the bill on the last day of the legislative session, convinced that it would be declared unconstitutional by the Tennessee Supreme Court.

Shortly thereafter, Nashville attorney John Vertrees filed a lawsuit challenging the new law's constitutionality. Vertrees was the husband of Virginia Vertrees, the president of the Tennessee chapter of the National Association Opposed to Woman Suffrage. More significantly, he owned a major distillery, and the liquor industry in Tennessee was strongly opposed to woman suffrage, forming an unholy alliance with the Women's Christian Temperance Union.

To the surprise of the governor, attorney Vertrees, the liquor industry, and sober female Christians across the state of Tennessee, the Tennessee Supreme Court dismissed the lawsuit.

Esther Hanover and women across the state of Tennessee now had the right to vote in presidential elections and municipal elections. They did not have the right to vote for governor, senator, or members of Congress.

But just a few weeks later, on June 4, 1919, the US Congress passed the proposed Nineteenth Amendment to the Constitution, subject to the approval of three quarters of the state legislatures, guaranteeing Esther Hanover and every woman in America the right to vote in all elections.

In a little over a year, the issue of woman suffrage would be back before the Tennessee legislature. This time Speaker Walker would have yet another change of heart, and many of the Tennessee legislators who had voted for partial suffrage would have a change of heart as well.

An epic constitutional battle would be decided in the state of Tennessee. And once again, Joseph Hanover would find himself right in the middle of it, but only after he won a fight to keep his seat in the legislature.

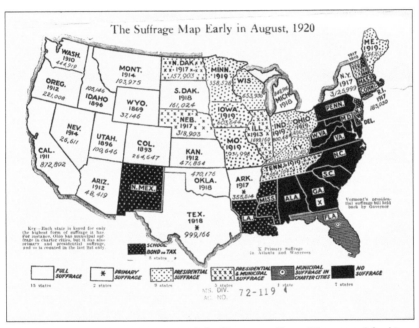

Photo courtesy of the Tennessee State Library and Archives

CLASS OF SERVICE | SYMBOL
Telegram |
Day Letter | Blue
Night Message | Nite
Night Letter | N L
If none of these three symbols appears after the check (number of words) this is a telegram. Otherwise its character is indicated by the symbol appearing after the check.

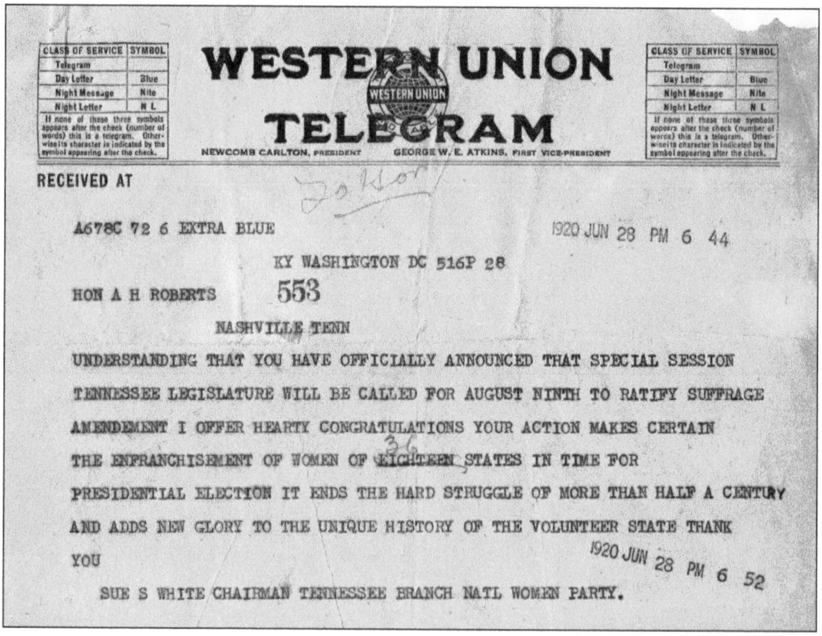

WESTERN UNION
TELEGRAM

NEWCOMB CARLTON, PRESIDENT GEORGE W. E. ATKINS, FIRST VICE-PRESIDENT

RECEIVED AT

A678C 72 6 EXTRA BLUE 1920 JUN 28 PM 6 44

KY WASHINGTON DC 516P 28

HON A H ROBERTS 553

NASHVILLE TENN

UNDERSTANDING THAT YOU HAVE OFFICIALLY ANNOUNCED THAT SPECIAL SESSION TENNESSEE LEGISLATURE WILL BE CALLED FOR AUGUST NINTH TO RATIFY SUFFRAGE AMENDMENT I OFFER HEARTY CONGRATULATIONS YOUR ACTION MAKES CERTAIN THE ENFRANCHISEMENT OF WOMEN OF EIGHTEEN STATES IN TIME FOR PRESIDENTIAL ELECTION IT ENDS THE HARD STRUGGLE OF MORE THAN HALF A CENTURY AND ADDS NEW GLORY TO THE UNIQUE HISTORY OF THE VOLUNTEER STATE THANK YOU

1920 JUN 28 PM 6 52

SUE S WHITE CHAIRMAN TENNESSEE BRANCH NATL WOMEN PARTY.

Photo courtesy of the Tennessee State Library and Archives

7

Removal
and Re-election

July 1st 1920.

Sue S. White, Chairman,
Tennessee Branch National Women Party,
Washington, D. C.

I wish to thank you sincerely for your telegram with reference to the
ratification of the nineteenth amendment   I have definitely announced that a special session of Legislature will be called to convene
August ninth   Official call to be issued at an early date and that
subject of ratification of nineteenth amendment will be included in the
call.

A. H. Roberts.

Photo courtesy of the Tennessee State Library and Archives

Whan the Tennessee General Assembly recessed in spring 1919, Joe Hanover was clearly a recognized star of the freshman class. Word soon spread around the state about his effectiveness as an advocate, particularly in his patriotic speeches on the floor of the Tennessee House of Representatives in favor of the passage of partial suffrage. He was also quickly establishing his reputation as an outstanding lawyer in the free legal advice and assistance he gave his colleagues in the legislature. The young independent was clearly on his way to becoming a powerful, major figure in the Tennessee General Assembly.

Hanover's work during his brief time in the legislature led to a new position, a real plum job for a young lawyer. In the spring of 1919, he was offered and accepted the position of assistant city attorney for Memphis. Just five years out of law school, he had both a prestigious legal position and a seat in the Tennessee legislature.

Then the attorney general of Tennessee threw him a legal curveball. On

August 1, 1919, Tennessee Attorney General Frank M. Thompson issued an opinion that Hanover and four other members of the Tennessee General Assembly were disqualified from continued service in the legislature. The attorney general opined that the Tennessee Constitution prohibited members of the legislature from accepting other public offices for pay, and since Hanover had become an assistant attorney for the city of Memphis, he could no longer serve in the General Assembly.

Hanover responded by ignoring the attorney general's opinion. He strongly disagreed with the attorney general's interpretation of the Constitution, and he regarded the issue as moot, at least for the foreseeable future. In that era, the Tennessee General Assembly convened only every other year. Having concluded the 61st General Assembly session in spring 1919, they were not scheduled to meet again until 1921. Besides, the attorney general had not removed Hanover from the legislature. He had simply issued an opinion with which Hanover disagreed.

But then the course of history made the issue no longer moot and more than just the opinion of a state attorney general.

As Hanover began his work as an assistant city attorney in Memphis, he could not help but notice what was happening across the nation. The proposed Nineteenth Amendment to the Constitution—guaranteeing full, not partial, suffrage to women—was proceeding state by state in legislatures across America.

Initially, states had lined up quickly for ratification with Wisconsin, Michigan, Kansas, Ohio, New York, and Illinois all approving it within an eight-day period following approval of the proposed Nineteenth Amendment by the US Congress.

But as the summer of 1919 wore on, resistance to ratification began to grow. The "Antis" mobilized, converging on state capitols and warning that ratification of the Nineteenth Amendment was "the first step towards socialism, free love, and the breakup of the American family."

Resistance was particularly strong in the South, as Louisiana Gov. Ruffin Pleasant publicly led a union of states across Dixie to oppose ratification. Six Southern states heeded the call by the Louisiana governor to reject the proposed amendment.

By New Year's Day in 1920, some twenty-two states had supported ratification, leaving fourteen states necessary to make the amendment a reality.

Hanover watched all this unfold and began to realize that the approval of the Nineteenth Amendment, delivering the right to vote to his mother and twenty-seven million other women across America, might come down to Tennessee.

By early summer 1920, thirty-five states had approved ratification of the Nineteenth Amendment. One more state was needed, but after a wave of rejections throughout the Deep South and in New England, the battle was coming down to two states—Delaware and Tennessee.

On June 2, 1920, the Delaware legislature rejected ratification of the Nineteenth Amendment.

More ominous news for the Suffs came from Ohio, one of the first states to act favorably on the proposed Nineteenth Amendment. A petition was circulating in the Buckeye State for a statewide referendum in which voters could either affirm or reject the legislature's ratification. The Antis were circulating similar petitions for post-ratification referenda in Missouri, Nebraska, Maine, and Massachusetts.

It was all coming down to the Volunteer State, and it was becoming increasingly clear that the 61st Tennessee General Assembly might be reconvened in a special session to decide the fate of the proposed Nineteenth Amendment. If there was going to be such an extraordinary session, Hanover did not intend to miss it, regardless of what the attorney general had said.

Then the governor of Tennessee forced the issue. On July 20, 1920, anticipating that he would soon call the legislature into extraordinary session, Governor Roberts issued a proclamation declaring that there were four vacancies in the legislature, including the position "formerly held by Joe Hanover." This irritated Hanover inasmuch as he had not resigned from the General Assembly. Nevertheless, the governor also declared that under his authority, a special election would be held on the fifth day of August to fill these vacancies.

On August 5, 1920, the voters in Shelby County District No. 5 went to the polls to elect a representative to assume the legislative seat that had been "vacated" by Hanover. When the votes were counted, the new representative was . . . Joe Hanover.

Upon hearing the news of the governor's proclamation, Hanover had done what he felt he had to do. He had resigned his position as Memphis assistant city attorney and filed to run for re-election to the legislative seat that the attorney general and the governor said he had vacated, and he had been re-elected easily.

On August 7, 1920, the governor issued another proclamation, this one calling the 61st Tennessee General Assembly into an extraordinary session to consider just one issue—the ratification of the proposed Nineteenth Amendment.

Hanover was heading back to Nashville, remembering the question he had asked his parents many years earlier: Why can't Mother vote?

Hanover was indeed ready to address some important unfinished business.

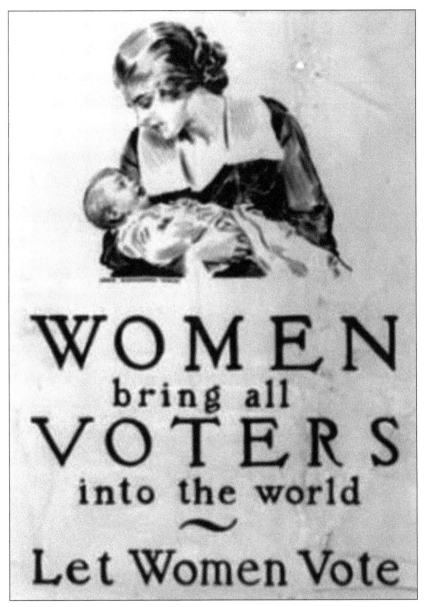

Carrie Chapman Catt

Photo courtesy of the Tennessee State Library and Archives
On August 8, 1920, Carrie Chapman Catt summoned Joe Hanover to her hotel suite. There she asked him to become the new floor leader in the Tennessee House of Representatives for the ratification of the Nineteenth Amendment.

8

A Summons
from Mrs. Catt

Nashville, Tenn., July 21, 1920.

Miss Evelyn Pegues,
Jackson, Tenn.

My dear Miss Pegues:-

If you think I can help you, I will willingly pay a visit to Knoxville. A luncheon, dinner, (Dutch treat) or late afternoon tea, might bring people together. All your legislators should be invited, and I will be glad to address any group you can collect; - the larger the better.

I am making this same offer to Memphis and suggesting that I go to them Monday next and should be glad to remain over Tuesday and go with their deputation if they so desire to see their men, and in that event I could be in Jackson Wednesday, and if you desire my help go with you to see some of your men and could remain over Thursday if you think it advisable.

Let me know if you think I can help and whether or not you find it possible to collect people in this hot July time.

I am only offering to go to Chattanooga, Memphis, Jackson and Knoxville.

Yours for victory,

CCC:MM.

Carrie Chapman Catt

Suite 309 Hermitage Hotel,
Nashville, Tenn.

Photo courtesy of Joan Tomlin of Jackson, Tennessee

Carrie Chapman Catt arrived in Nashville on July 17, 1920, to gather the pro-suffrage forces and began her letters, appeals, and appearances. This letter went to Evelyn Pegues of Jackson and concerns public appearances in Memphis, Jackson, Chattanooga, and Knoxville.

On July 17, 1920, Carrie Chapman Catt arrived in Nashville and checked into a suite at The Hermitage Hotel. The silver-haired, twice-widowed sixty-year-old was in her second term as president of the National American Woman Suffrage Association, selected as president in 1900 by none other than Susan B. Anthony.

It was not Mrs. Catt's first visit to the beautiful hotel. Six years earlier, in 1914, Mrs. Catt had attended the National American Woman Suffrage Association Convention, which had been held at The Hermitage Hotel under the direction of Anne Dallas Dudley, president of the Nashville Equal Suffrage League and wife of Guilford Dudley, president of Nashville's Life and Casualty Insurance Company.

Catt had spent the last four years of her life crisscrossing the United States, leading her "Winning Plan" in pursuit of suffrage. The plan sought support for suffrage at both the state and federal levels, including a pursuit of partial suffrage in the states most resistant to a proposed federal suffrage amendment.

Catt was exhausted. She planned to be in Nashville for only a few days, bringing with her just one small traveling bag. She thought she was in the home stretch of the seventy-two-year-old battle to win women the right to vote, and she firmly believed that Tennessee was about to become the "Perfect 36," the thirty-sixth and final state that would ratify the proposed Nineteenth Amendment and make it part of the Constitution of the United States.

She had every reason to be optimistic. Proposed ratification of the Nineteenth Amendment had the support of Tennessee Governor Roberts (who had overcome his earlier reluctance), Tennessee House Speaker Seth Walker, and even Boss Crump in Memphis. Sen. Kenneth D. McKellar was sending word of support from Washington, including letters from President Woodrow Wilson with an eye on the upcoming 1920 presidential election.

It was anticipated that once the Tennessee primary elections were over in early August, Governor Roberts would call for a special session of the Tennessee legislature to quickly pass the proposed constitutional amendment. Ratification appeared to be imminent as some sixty-two House members and twenty-five state senators had signed pledges promising their support.

And then, to Catt's horror, the support for ratification of the Nineteenth Amendment in the Volunteer State began to unravel.

On the same day that Catt checked into The Hermitage Hotel, another strong-willed woman arrived there. Josephine Anderson Pearson of Monteagle, Tennessee, president of the Tennessee Association Opposed to Woman Suffrage, arrived at the hotel and requested the cheapest room available. But she also rented the hotel's mezzanine assembly rooms as campaign headquarters for the Antis.

Pearson and her Anti forces began passing out handbills in the hotel lobby that read, "Beware, men of the South, and heed not the suffrage siren!"

Pearson then began to put together a coalition consisting of lawyers who argued that ratification of the proposed amendment violated the Tennessee Constitution, states' rights advocates, evangelical preachers, the L&N Railroad, and some strange political bedfellows—liquor lobbyists and members of the Women's Christian Temperance Union.

Unfortunately, underlying all of the Antis' arguments was the race question. While black citizens in Memphis regularly voted thanks to the support of Boss Crump and his machine (who even paid black voters' poll taxes), in most of Tennessee the Jim Crow laws enacted at the end of Reconstruction kept black folks from going to the polls. The Antis warned that if women were given the right to vote, black people would be voting as well. Antis proclaimed that giving women the right to vote would "blacken the honor of Robert E. Lee."

Josephine Anderson Pearson organized an Anti mass rally at the Grand Ole Opry's Ryman Auditorium. This was followed by a series of Anti prayer meetings at churches across the state of Tennessee.

Catt herself left The Hermitage Hotel for a few days, motoring across the state to deliver pro-suffrage speeches to the Memphis Chamber of Commerce, the Rotary Club, the Nashville Kiwanis Club, and at citizens meetings in Jackson, Knoxville, and Chattanooga.

On Sunday, July 25, the Tennessee League of Women Voters announced that its latest legislative poll, based on signed pledges from members, showed an assured majority for ratification in both houses.

But the resistance to suffrage across the state of Tennessee continued to grow, and Catt was worried.

On Thursday, August 5, Governor Roberts won the Democratic primary, nominating him for re-election. Two days later, on Saturday, August 7, just as he had promised, the governor issued a proclamation calling the 61st General Assembly into an extraordinary session at noon on the following Monday to debate and vote on the ratification of the Nineteenth Amendment.

That weekend, 123 members of the Tennessee General Assembly arrived in Nashville, and most of them checked into The Hermitage Hotel's 250 rooms or the nearby Maxwell House or Tulane Hotel. Joe Hanover got his room on the third floor, just down the hall from Catt's suite.

Hundreds of women arrived as well, donning either yellow roses for suffrage or red roses against suffrage. The national media also arrived to cover Tennessee's "War of the Roses," with the prospect of twenty-seven million American women voting in the upcoming presidential election.

The battle lines were drawn in yellow and red.

If the sixty-two pledges in the House of Representatives and the twenty-five pledges in the state Senate would hold, ratification was assured. But then one of those pledges vanished, and it was perhaps the most significant pledge of all.

Tennessee House Speaker Walker, who had been against woman suffrage before he was in favor of it, suddenly had another conversion.

Prior to the convening of the extraordinary session, Speaker Walker had agreed that he would introduce the resolution of ratification to the House himself, virtually assuring its passage.

But on Sunday morning, August 8, Speaker Walker appeared in the Capitol House Caucus Room and advised aides to Governor Roberts that he had "undergone a change of conviction." Just a year earlier, Walker had spoken passionately on the floor of the House in support of partial suffrage for Tennessee women. But now, with no explanation, he told the governor's assistants that it would be political disaster for the governor and legislative leaders to support the ratification of the Nineteenth Amendment.

When he walked out of the Caucus Room that morning, the word of his conversion quickly spread to his fellow legislators, and suddenly it appeared that many formerly pledged votes were also about to become born-again Antis.

Legislators began to convene at the "Jack Daniel's Suite" on the eighth floor of the hotel, imbibing anti-Suff bourbon and moonshine whiskey.

Many legislators spent all night in the "Jack Daniel's Suite," literally threatening the sobriety of the General Assembly. Catt was appalled as Suffs who had attempted to lobby legislators reported that the legislators they approached were often either drunk or hung over. There was even concern that they might not be able to convene a quorum to vote on the Nineteenth Amendment in the House.

Catt asked Nashville law enforcement why Prohibition was not enforced. "Now see here," came the answer. "In Tennessee, whiskey and legislation go hand in hand, especially when controversial questions are urged. . . . This is the Tennessee way!"

Suffs Sue Shelton White and Anita Pollitzer tried to eavesdrop on the goings-on in the "Jack Daniel's Suite." The anti-Suff Chattanooga Times learned of their efforts and ran a front-page story under the blazing headline "TWO WOMEN SPIES CAUGHT IN HOTEL."

The Antis were offering not only liquor but money as well. Bribes were being offered, and there was even a rumor that lobbyists for certain railroad interests had made lucrative promises to Speaker Walker, leading to his latest conversion on the suffrage issue. He angrily denied this. A couple of years later, after leaving the Tennessee legislature, he became general counsel to a railroad company.

Catt began to have nightly strategy sessions in her suite, room 309. One of the legislators who attended every session was Joe Hanover of Memphis. Catt listened to Hanover's earnest arguments in favor of suffrage, and she was impressed. She also heard the stories about how the rural legislators in particular respected Hanover and appreciated the legal assistance this bright young lawyer gave them.

The floor leader for the fight in the House of Representatives for passage of woman suffrage had been Rep. T. K. Riddick, a Memphis attorney. Riddick was an able lawyer, but his rural colleagues in the House regarded him as "high-falutin'." He came across to them as arrogant and condescending.

Catt heard these stories as well, as the pledged numbers for ratification dropped from sixty-two down to fifty-two and then even perilously close to falling below the fifty-vote majority required for passage.

Catt made a decision. On Wednesday evening, August 8, she summoned Hanover to her suite, where she asked him to become the new floor leader in the Tennessee House of Representatives for the passage of the Nineteenth Amendment.

Hanover was surprised by the request, but he immediately agreed.

He had come to Nashville that hot and humid August to fulfill a promise that he, in effect, had made to his mother long ago, and he was going to see it through.

Photo courtesy of the Tennessee State Library and Archives
'Truth crushed to the earth will rise again' is illustrated in this photo
of anti-suffragists who unsuccessfully sought to prevent ratification of
the Nineteenth Amendment.

9

The Battle of the
Women of Faith

MISS LIZZIE LEE BLOOMSTEIN.

Photo courtesy of the Tennessee State Library and Archives
Elizabeth Lee Bloomstein, who was a member of one
of Nashville's most prominent Jewish families, became
a leading voice for suffrage. A seminarian, history
professor at George Peabody College, and leader of
the National Federation of Women's Clubs, 'Lizzie'
Bloomstein led a coalition of women's organizations in
support of the suffrage cause.

As Joe Hanover prepared to assume the leadership of the legislative battle for ratification of the Nineteenth Amendment, unique battle lines were being drawn in the "War of the Roses." It was becoming in large measure a battle between women of faith. Josephine Pearson was the daughter of a Methodist minister. She herself taught at Christian colleges and later became the president of a seminary.

For Josephine Pearson and many of her red-rose-wearing sisters, the issue of woman suffrage was not simply a political or legal one. It was a moral issue. As a fundamentalist Christian, Josephine Pearson believed the Bible was the word of God. From her reading of it, God was clearly opposed to woman suffrage. Pearson would cite the words of the apostle Paul as if he were writing not only to the Romans, the Corinthians, and the Thessalonians, but also to the members of the Tennessee legislature. Paul wrote that women should be silent and "graciously submissive" to men, deferring all authority to men.

Josephine Pearson did not remain silent. She was outspoken in her belief that woman suffrage was contrary to God's word and to the role the Almighty wanted women to fulfill in their families and by supporting the leadership of men in their churches and the community.

Pearson was also outspoken in her belief that the women who supported suffrage were, for the most part, atheists. Her primary evidence of this was *The Woman's Bible*, a book written in 1896 by the noted suffragist Elizabeth Cady Stanton and a committee of twenty-six women, challenging the traditional faith view of the role of women as subservient to men.

Almost immediately after its publication, the book was denounced by Stanton's best friend, Susan B. Anthony, and by suffragists who saw it as undermining support for the cause of women's equal rights in general and the right to vote in particular.

Carrie Chapman Catt sought to dissociate the suffrage movement from the controversial book, but nearly a quarter century after its publication, Josephine Pearson and the Antis were citing *The Woman's Bible* to Christian members of the Tennessee General Assembly as evidence that the Suffs were literally trying to rewrite God's word.

But the yellow-rose-adorned sisters included many women of faith who saw their cause as a holy one. They read the Bible as a call for justice, quoting the prophet Amos, who said, "Let justice roll on like a river, righteousness like a never-failing stream," and the prophet Micah: "What does the Lord require of you? To act justly and to love mercy and to walk humbly with your God."

The suffragist movement had its roots in the 1840s with the abolitionist movement, as Christian women sought to abolish slavery. The Holiness movement of the late nineteenth century inspired many Christian women to support social reform in the context of race relations, child welfare, and ultimately woman suffrage.

Even conservative women who believed in the traditional roles of women and families saw votes by women as a chance to elect men who would support education, public health, safe working conditions, and the protection of children.

The yellow rose Christian women of faith who gathered, marched, and lobbied in Nashville in August 1920 in support of suffrage were joined by other sisters of faith, specifically their Jewish sisters.

Jewish women in Nashville had been working diligently for the cause of woman suffrage in the years leading up to the culminating vote in the Tennessee legislature in August 1920.

In 1912, the Nashville Equal Suffrage League was formed. Charter members Agnes Kuhn and Sarah Lowenstein Teitlebaum gave faithful voices to the cause of votes for women. The Council of Jewish Women's Auxiliary, under the leadership of Lettie Lusky, joined the campaign.

In 1915, Helen Wile Mills led a May Day suffrage rally in downtown Nashville.

Elizabeth Lee Bloomstein, a member of one of Nashville's most prominent Jewish families, became a leading voice for suffrage. A seminarian, history professor at George Peabody College, and leader of the National Federation of Women's Clubs, "Lizzie" Bloomstein led a coalition of women's organizations in support of the suffrage cause. The alliance included the Ladies Hermitage Association, the Tennessee Women's Press Club, and the Women's Historical Association.

In August 1920, the overwhelming majority of members of the Tennessee House of Representatives were Christians, most sharing the evangelical background of Josephine Pearson. But in working for the passage of the Nineteenth Amendment, Joseph Hanover, a practicing Orthodox Jew, had the support of a coalition of women of diverse faith backgrounds.

The faithful Suff sisters did agree with Josephine Pearson on one important point: The issue of woman suffrage was indeed a moral one.

Photo courtesy of the Tennessee State Library and Archives

10

'You're a Pretty Cheap Vote— They Are Paying Others a Thousand!'

Photo courtesy of the Tennessee State Library and Archives

On the morning after he had agreed to become the floor leader for ratification, Rep. Joe Hanover expressed confidence that Tennessee would soon become the "Perfect 36" state. "There is absolutely no chance of defeat," he told the *Washington Morning Star*. "The resolution will be passed by a liberal majority."

Despite his optimism, Hanover faced a number of issues as he approached his fellow legislators who had previously pledged support for ratification but were now, at the very least, wavering, sometimes literally, as they left the "Jack Daniel's Suite."

One of the first issues was "vote trading." That was a euphemism for outright bribery. The well-funded lobbyists for the liquor, railroad, and business interests opposing woman suffrage were approaching legislators previously pledged to ratification and simply buying Seth Walker-like conversions.

Catt had not given Hanover any funds to engage in his own vote trading. Even if such funds were available, Hanover's integrity would have prevented him from buying votes. Instead, he had to rely on his cunning and skills as a lawyer.

Early one morning, one of his colleagues in the House, an old, fiddle-playing farmer from the hills of East Tennessee, knocked on Joe's hotel room door. He was one of the many rural legislators whom Hanover had assisted with legal issues and in drafting proposed bills, and he had been an ardent supporter of the proposed ratification of woman suffrage. But he apologized, announcing, "Sorry, Joe, but I'm going to leave you suffrage boys. The Antis just paid me $300."

Hanover immediately responded, "Well, you're a pretty cheap vote—I hear they are paying others a thousand."

"Why, those dirty crooks!" cried the fiddle-playing farmer. He assured Hanover that he would not only vote for ratification, but he would tell his colleagues in the House of the "wickedness" of the Antis.

The second issue Hanover had to address was a legal one. Speaker Walker was warning his colleagues that if they voted for ratification, they would be violating their oath to uphold the Tennessee Constitution. Walker cited a provision of the Tennessee Constitution requiring that any proposed federal amendment be acted upon only by a legislature that "shall have been elected after such amendment is submitted." The speaker argued that this meant that the proposed Nineteenth Amendment could only be approved by a Tennessee legislature elected after the 1920 elections.

Lawyer Joe Hanover thoughtfully pointed out to his colleagues that the US Supreme Court had addressed this issue two months earlier in a case involving a similar state constitutional provision in Ohio. The Supreme Court had declared, "The Federal Constitution, and not the Constitutions of the several states, controls the method by which the US Constitution may be amended."

In case his colleagues in the House were states-righters who wished to disregard a ruling of the US Supreme Court, Hanover had secured an opinion from Tennessee Attorney General Frank M. Thompson, the same attorney general who had declared Hanover's legislative seat vacated, which stated unequivocally that "there was no legal barrier" to the current Tennessee legislature voting on ratification of the proposed constitutional amendment.

Then Hanover had to respond to a myriad of arguments raised by the Antis.

There was the ironic argument that giving women the right to vote would pull them off their pedestals, demean them, and drag them into the surly world of politics.

The Antis warned that woman suffrage threatened the traditional American family, as women would not only vote but would leave the home and hearth, putting their children in institutions or, perish the thought, asking husbands to share childcare duties.

Antis also claimed that giving women the right to vote would threaten the American legal system, in particular the right of trials by jury. Once women started voting, they would be serving on juries, bringing their "irrational and emotional thoughts" to deliberations. There would no longer be twelve angry men. It would be twelve emotional women.

In speeches on the floor of the House of Representatives and in one-on-one meetings with his fellow legislators, Hanover responded with a heartfelt tribute to his mother and to all women of America.

He said as an immigrant growing up in his new country, he could not understand why women were denied the constitutional right to vote. He proudly recalled the intelligence, strength, and wisdom of his mother. He said those attributes were shared by millions of American women. And then he told his fellow legislators that they should vote for woman suffrage not only for the sake of women but to make America a stronger and better country.

"A mother brings a child into this world but has no say afterward about the future of that child, his education, or rearing," he argued. Voting women would support better schools and cleaner and more honest government.

He also cited the tireless work of millions of American women on behalf of their nation during the recent world war. He fondly quoted Nashville suffragist Anne Dallas Dudley: "Men may bear arms, but women bear armies!"

Then Hanover had to respond to the race question, specifically the Antis' dire warning that giving women the right to vote would open the ballot boxes to blacks as well.

Carrie Chapman Catt was no racist. She spent her life fighting for the rights of all Americans. But in a Machiavellian move, in response to a reporter's question, she had said, "White supremacy will not be threatened by women's suffrage."

Hanover made no such argument. Instead he responded with patriotism. Hanover said he was no liberal. He was a true conservative. And as a true conservative, he believed in the Bill of Rights and that the precious rights set forth therein should be afforded to all Americans. He told the story of his own journey to America, across a frozen lake and then across the sea, to escape tyranny and oppression. The right to vote was at the heart of what made America great.

Hanover paid a heavy price for his tireless work as legislative leader in the fight for woman suffrage. The phone in his room at the hotel rang throughout the night and into the early morning hours. When he would answer it, he would either hear male voices threatening his life or cooing female voices asking him to come to their rooms to get their support. At first Joe laughed off the threats from the male voices and the obvious traps that were being set up by the female ones.

But then he was physically assaulted and beaten in the hotel elevator by a stranger screaming that Joe was a "Bolshevik" and a "Kike."

After hearing about the assault, Governor Roberts summoned Joe to his office in the Capitol and introduced him to Capt. Paul Bush, who would serve as Joe's bodyguard. Joe resisted, but the governor's insistence allowed Captain Bush to accompany Joe at The Hermitage Hotel and on Capitol Hill.

During the extraordinary session, Hanover lost twenty pounds and developed an ulcer. But he had left his position as assistant city attorney in Memphis and returned to Nashville to fulfill what he saw as an awesome responsibility to his own mother and to millions of her "sisters" across America.

"Why wave the bloody shirt between North and South when we all went across the seas together?"

Rep. Joe Hanover responding to Tennessee House Speaker Seth Walker

Joe Hanover told the state House of Representatives: 'Tennessee never does things by halves for women. What we do for them as Southern men we should now have the privilege of doing for other women ... that ours may be truly a democracy.'

11

'A White Man's Country!'

A Suffrage Timetable, Country by Country

At the moment Tennessee's ratification of the Nineteenth Amendment to the US Constitution granted American women the right to vote, woman suffrage had already become a reality in twenty-six other countries—beginning, fittingly enough, with the Isle of Man, in 1881. This chronological listing, country by country and year by year, of the order in which women were enfranchised, was reported in the *New York Times* on August 19, 1920.

1. Isle of Man	1881	14. Poland	1918
2. New Zealand	1893	15. Scotland	1918
3. Australia	1902	16. Austria	1918
4. Finland	1906	17. Czechoslovakia	1918
5. Norway	1907	18. Hungary	1918
6. Denmark	1915	19. Holland	1919
7. Mexico	1917	20. British East Africa	1919
8. Russia	1917	21. Luxemburg	1919
9. Ireland	1918	22. Uruguay	1919
10. Wales	1918	23. Belgium	1919
11. Canada	1918	24. Rhodesia	1919
12. Germany	1918	25. Iceland	1919
13. England	1918	26. Sweden	1919

On Tuesday, August 17, 1920, the Tennessee House of Representatives met for what would be the final debate on the ratification of the proposed Nineteenth Amendment to the Constitution of the United States. The state Senate had already approved the resolution for ratification overwhelmingly by a 25–4 vote.

For ten days, the legislators had convened in the sweltering heat of a Tennessee August. And now the decision day had finally arrived.

The decision would be made by the House.

The debate began with a public reading of a telegram from President Woodrow Wilson urging the Tennessee representatives to approve suffrage. This was greeted with thunderous applause from hundreds of women in the gallery wearing yellow roses on their white dresses.

Then House Speaker Seth Walker turned over his gavel to the speaker pro tem. He came down onto the floor of the House and proceeded to make his final argument on the issue of woman suffrage.

Speaker Walker had spoken on the issue only one year earlier, during consideration of partial suffrage. At that time, he had spoken affirmatively of giving Negroes the right to vote and contended that the right should be given to women as well.

But now he turned that argument on its head. "This is a moral issue," he began. "We want this to remain a white man's country!"

He read a letter purportedly from the "Los Angeles Colored Ladies Club" urging support of the proposed Nineteenth Amendment so "colored ladies" could vote.

Pausing for effect, Walker then shouted, "I say this is infamous!"

At that point, there were cheers from the women in the gallery who were wearing red roses.

Speaker Walker had made it perfectly clear what he thought was at stake in the upcoming vote. It was the Tennessean way of life . . . the white male Tennesseans' way of life.

Then it was time for Joe Hanover to respond. "Ours is the great Volunteer State," he began. "Women from east, west, north, and south are looking to us to give them political freedom . . . the entire world has cast its eyes on Tennessee. This is a moral question, and that's why I'm here voting for this amendment."

He directly responded to Speaker Walker's racist rant. "Why wave the bloody shirt between North and South," he asked, "when we all went across the seas together?"

He reiterated his own story . . . the story of a young man whose father had brought him, his mother, and his brothers to America to escape oppression.

He closed on a deeply patriotic note by saying, "Tennessee never does things by halves for women. What we do for them as Southern men we should now have the privilege of doing for other women . . . that ours may be truly a democracy."

At the conclusion of Hanover's final argument for woman suffrage, the yellow-rose-clad Suffs in the House gallery erupted with deafening cheers. But while those cheers rained down, Speaker Walker, still on the House floor, asked to be recognized. "I move this House adjourn till tomorrow morning," he announced.

"No! No!" shouted Hanover, concerned that further delay would give the Antis more time to convert previously pledged Suffs with persuasion and, if necessary, intimidation, booze, and bribes.

Hanover wanted the vote for ratification of the Nineteenth Amendment immediately. But Speaker Walker's motion to adjourn passed by a vote of 52–44. The vote to adjourn heightened Hanover's concerns that Walker and the Antis were closing in on the fifty votes to defeat the amendment.

That evening, Hanover returned to Catt's suite at the hotel for a final Suff strategy session. The mood was somber as the latest poll showed the majority in the House for passage of the amendment had disappeared. The Suffs were two votes short.

As the meeting ended, a despondent Catt whispered, "There is one more thing we can do. We can pray."

Photo courtesy of the Tennessee State Library and Archives

12

'The Hour Has Come'

Photo courtesy of the Tennessee State Library and Archives

On the following morning, August 18, 1920, Nashville police estimated that more than forty thousand people had gathered outside the Capitol. The "War of the Roses" was about to have its final battle.

At ten thirty, Speaker Walker pounded his gavel to bring the House to order. It took some time for the sergeant at arms to accomplish this, as the House floor was covered with Suffs, Antis, and dozens of lobbyists who were making last-minute offers and appeals.

Joe Hanover worked the floor, moving from one legislative colleague to another and whispering in their ears.

There was a flyer on the desk of each House delegate, placed there by the Antis. It wasn't subtle. It read, "The better class of NEGROES THEMSELVES know they are better represented by able white men than they would be by designating politicians of their own race, just as the majority of women themselves feel they are better represented by the fathers of their children than they would be by politically ambitious office seekers of their own sex."

Many had anticipated that there would be further prolonged debate on the proposed resolution for ratification. But Speaker Walker quickly cut this off. Handing the gavel to Speaker Pro Tem Austin Overton, he stepped down onto the floor. "The hour has come," he announced. "The battle has been fought and won, and I move . . . that the motion to concur in the Senate action go where it belongs—to the table."

Speaker Walker was moving to kill the proposed ratification of the Nineteenth Amendment by tabling the resolution.

Anti-Suff legislators screamed, "Second the motion!" Hanover clamored for recognition.

The Antis had spread the word that voting to table the resolution was not a vote against woman suffrage. It was an opportunity for the voters in the upcoming election to say whether they supported woman suffrage. All male voters, that is. Since there were campaigns underway in other state legislatures to rescind previous ratifications of the Nineteenth Amendment, the motion to table was in reality a motion to defeat woman suffrage.

The roll call began, and at first there were no surprises. Every delegate was voting as anticipated. Rep. Harry Burn, donning a red rose, voted to table.

Then the name Banks Turner was called. While Turner was not wearing a red rose, he was known to be a committed Anti.

When Turner's name was first called, he did not respond. The roll call went on, but before the final vote could be announced, Turner rose and said, "I wish to be recorded as against the motion to table." Suffs gasped in joy. Antis screamed in protest. Turner's surprise vote made the final count 48–48, a tie, defeating the motion to table. The Nineteenth Amendment was still alive.

Speaker Walker was convinced that Turner had simply made a mistake. He demanded a recount and then made his way to Turner's desk, sat down beside him, and put his arm around Turner's shoulder. But when Turner's name was called again, he threw off Walker's arm, rose, and again voted, "Nay."

What Walker did not know was that earlier that morning, Turner had been summoned to the office of Governor Roberts. Sitting across the desk from the governor, he heard a long-distance phone conversation that Governor Roberts was having with another governor . . . Gov. James Cox of Ohio, the Democratic nominee for president of the United States. Governor Cox was pleading with

Governor Roberts to make sure the Tennessee legislature approved the Nineteenth Amendment of the Constitution of the United States, as it would mean that twenty-seven million American women could vote in the upcoming presidential election and help put Governor Cox into the White House.

Directly facing Banks Turner, Governor Roberts had responded to Governor Cox by saying, "The man who can make this happen is sitting across from me."

Turner had left the governor's office that morning quietly deciding that he would support ratification, but he told no one.

After the second vote on the motion to table failed, again in a 48–48 tie, Walker did not hesitate. He was certain that as the motion to table had failed on a tie vote, a motion to concur with the Senate's ratification of the Nineteenth Amendment would do likewise. Walker immediately called for a vote on ratification. The hour had indeed come.

The roll call began. The first six votes called went exactly as expected, with two "ayes" and four "nays." Hanover's heart pounded as he realized that he needed two more votes for ratification–Turner's and one more.

And then the name Harry Burn was called. Just moments before, the red-rose-wearing Burn had voted twice to table suffrage. But this time when Burn's name was called, he said, "Aye." His vote came so quickly and unexpectedly that many on the floor of the legislature did not catch it. But Walker did, and so did Hanover. Walker was convinced that Burn had simply made a mistake, just as he had thought Turner had done on the motion to table.

Shortly thereafter, the name Banks Turner was called. Walker was still on the floor, standing by Turner's desk, glaring at him. But Turner did not hesitate. He shouted, "Aye!"

Moments later, the gallery erupted. The motion to approve ratification of the Nineteenth Amendment of the Constitution of the United States had carried, 49–47.

There was pandemonium on the House floor as Hanover and Burn were swarmed by both Suffs and Antis.

Hanover was concerned about Burn's safety, but Burn escaped the Capitol through an anteroom beside the House floor. What both Hanover and Walker would later learn was that when Burn came to the Capitol that day, he was wearing a red rose on the outside of his suit coat. But in a pocket inside that suit coat was a note from his mother. The handwritten note said:

> *"Dear Son: Hurrah and vote for suffrage and don't keep them in doubt. . . . Don't forget to be a good boy and help Mrs. Catt. . . . Lots of love, Mama."*

Burn had read the note and had done what his mother had asked him to do.

Walker then played one more parliamentary hand. "I change my vote from 'nay' to 'aye,' and move to reconsider," he said.

Only a legislator voting on the prevailing side could bring up a motion to reconsider. Under House rules, the speaker then had seventy-two hours to call for a vote on the motion to reconsider in one last maneuver to defeat the proposed constitutional amendment.

Ironically, in changing his vote, Walker had actually given the ratification resolution an unchallengeable constitutional majority. It now had a total vote of fifty of the ninety-nine members of the House. Walker had cut off the sole line of legal attack upon Tennessee's ratification of the Nineteenth Amendment.

A few blocks away, with the windows open in her suite at The Hermitage Hotel, Carrie Chapman Catt heard the cheers from the Suffs pouring out of the Capitol, triumphantly throwing their yellow roses into the air.

Catt realized what had happened. But she correctly sensed that the battle was not over.

VOTES FOR WOMEN

On August 18, 1920, Tennessee became the 36th state to ratify the 19th Amendment to the U. S. Constitution, thereby giving all American women the right to vote. After weeks of intense lobbying by national leaders, Tennessee passed the measure by one vote. The headquarters for both suffragists, wearing yellow roses, and anti-suffragists, wearing red roses, were in the Hermitage Hotel.

DONATED IN MEMORY OF CARLEEN B. WALLER
THE HISTORICAL COMMISSION OF METROPOLITAN NASHVILLE AND DAVIDSON COUNTY

NO. 84   ERECTED 1999

Tennessee State Library and Archives/Photo by William M. Thomas
A historic marker outside The Hermitage Hotel in downtown Nashville commemorates the victory of the suffragists on August 18, 1920, in winning the vote for ratification of the Nineteenth Amendment.

Mass Meeting
TONIGHT

Ryman Auditorium
8 O'CLOCK
TO SAVE THE SOUTH

**FROM THE SUSAN B. ANTHONY AMENDMENT
AND FEDERAL SUFFRAGE FORCE BILLS**

Senator Oscar W. Underwood, of Alabama, and Ex-Gov. Ruffin G. Pleasant,
of Louisiana, Have Been Invited to Speak

MAJ. E. B. STAHLMAN
MISS CHARLOTTE E. ROWE
HON. FRANK P. BOND
AND
PROF. GUS DYER
WILL SPEAK
MRS. THOMAS H. MALONE, JR.
WILL SING
JUDGE J. C. HIGGINS
WILL PRESIDE

EVERYBODY INVITED

False Affidavits and the Red Rose Brigade Heads for Alabama

On Saturday, August 21, 1920, at three in the morning, Charl Ormond Williams, vice chairman of the Democratic National Committee and pro-suffrage leader, called Joe Hanover in tears to tell him that a group of the anti-Suff representatives had boarded a train early that morning and fled to Decatur, Alabama. As passengers on the Red Rose Brigade, they were attempting to thwart the Tennessee legislature having a quorum in the ratification process.

The Antis held a series of closed-door meetings in the hours after the vote to approve ratification of the Nineteenth Amendment had passed the House. They announced that they would have a mass meeting at Nashville's Ryman Auditorium on the following evening, under the theme "To Save the South." They also launched a campaign to have hundreds of telegrams sent to legislators urging them to support the motion to reconsider. All they needed to do was change one vote.

Then the Antis came up with another strategy, a devious one. They developed a story, claiming that just moments before the vote, Joe Hanover had dragged poor Harry Burn by his red-rose-adorned lapels into a side room of the chamber, roughed him up, and offered him a bribe of $10,000 to vote for ratification.

The Antis even came up with signed affidavits from "witnesses" claiming they had seen this sordid episode occur.

That evening, representatives from the Antis approached both Hanover and Burn and warned them if they did not vote for reconsideration on the following day, the Antis would unleash the documents to tell the public of how Hanover had, in effect, kidnapped Burn and then bribed him to secure his vote.

Both Burn and Hanover were outraged in the face of such blackmail.

The following morning, the *Nashville Tennessean* newspaper covered the story and exposed the affidavits from the "witnesses" as fraudulent. As it turned out, the stenographer who had been hired to take the dictation for the affidavits was a committed Suff. As she took the dictation, she also wrote the statements of the "witnesses" and their co-conspirators admitting that their testimony was bogus. She transcribed all of this and handed it over to a reporter from the *Nashville Tennessean*.

The story was quickly and totally discounted.

That morning, Burn, Hanover, and Turner all walked into the chambers of the Tennessee House of Representatives to a tumultuous ovation from the galleries. Burn asked Speaker Walker for permission to make a statement. Burn then stated, "I desire to resent in the name of honesty and justice the veiled intimidation and accusation regarding my vote on the Suffragist Amendment as indicated in certain statements, and it is my sincere belief that those responsible for their existence know that there is not a scintilla of truth in them."

He went on to say, "I want to state that I changed my vote in favor of ratification first because I believe in full suffrage as a right; I believe we had a moral and legal right to ratify, and I knew that a mother's advice is always safest for a boy to follow, and my mother wanted me to vote for ratification."

Realizing that he did not have the votes to pass his motion for reconsideration, Seth Walker managed to postpone the vote for a day or two.

Then the Antis made a last desperate move. They fled Nashville.

On Saturday, August 21, at three o'clock in the morning, Hanover was awakened by a phone call. When he answered the phone, he did not hear a male voice threatening to kill him. He did hear a female voice, but it was not one of those voices he had heard before offering to meet him and give him "support." Instead, it was the voice of suffragist Charl Ormond Williams. In tears, she told him that a group of the anti-Suff representatives had boarded a train early that morning and fled to Decatur, Alabama. As passengers on the "Red Rose Brigade," they were attempting to thwart the legislature having a quorum in the ratification process.

Hanover laughed. He reassured Williams that she should not worry. He told her it was, in fact, a criminal offense for a legislator to leave the House with the deliberate intention of breaking a quorum. "If necessary," he said, "I will see that they are arrested and forced to return."

It was not necessary.

When the legislature convened the following morning, forty-eight legislators who had voted for suffrage were present, along with Speaker Walker and eight anti-Suff legislators. There was a quorum.

The House quickly voted to table the motion to reconsider and then reaffirmed their previous vote for ratification and sent the bill to Governor Roberts's desk for his certification.

The seventy-two-year battle was finally over.

Gov. A. H. Roberts signs Tennessee's ratification of the Nineteenth Amendment on August 24, 1920.

14

Signed, Sealed, and Delivered

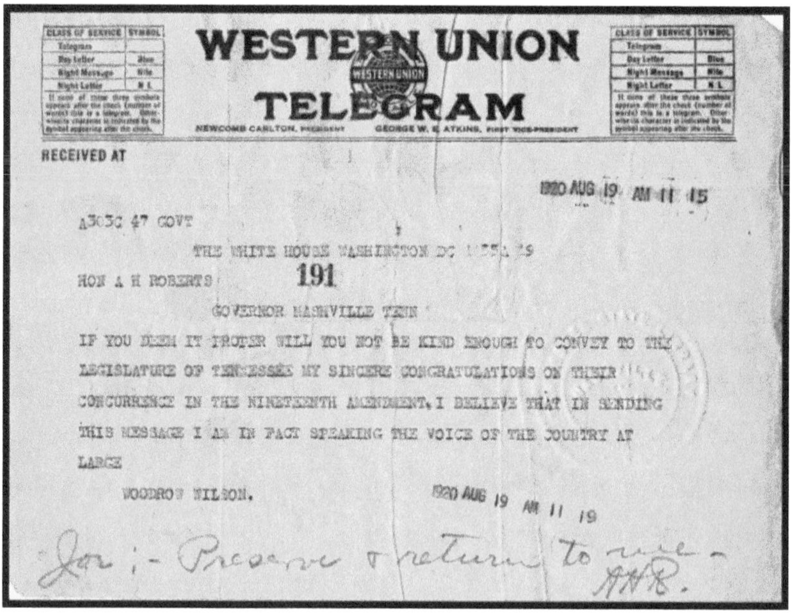

WESTERN UNION TELEGRAM

NEWCOMB CARLTON, PRESIDENT — GEORGE W. E. ATKINS, FIRST VICE-PRESIDENT

CLASS OF SERVICE	SYMBOL
Telegram	
Day Letter	Blue
Night Message	Nite
Night Letter	N L

If none of these three symbols appears after the check (number of words) this is a telegram. Otherwise its character is indicated by the symbol appearing after the check.

RECEIVED AT

1920 AUG 19 AM 11 15

A303C 47 GOVT

THE WHITE HOUSE WASHINGTON DC [illegible]

HON A H ROBERTS 191

GOVERNOR NASHVILLE TENN

IF YOU DEEM IT PROPER WILL YOU NOT BE KIND ENOUGH TO CONVEY TO THE LEGISLATURE OF TENNESSEE MY SINCERE CONGRATULATIONS ON THEIR CONCURRENCE IN THE NINETEENTH AMENDMENT. I BELIEVE THAT IN SENDING THIS MESSAGE I AM IN FACT SPEAKING THE VOICE OF THE COUNTRY AT LARGE

WOODROW WILSON.

1920 AUG 19 AM 11 19

Joe; - Preserve & return to me - AHR.

Library of Congress

On Tuesday, August 24, Governor Roberts signed the certificate of Tennessee's ratification of the Nineteenth Amendment. He sealed it and sent it off by special delivery, registered mail to US Secretary of State Bainbridge Colby in Washington, DC.

On the following morning, Carrie Chapman Catt checked out of room 309 of The Hermitage Hotel and headed for Nashville's Union Station. Joining her were her sister suffragists Harriet Upton, Marjorie Shuler, and Charl Ormond Williams. They boarded a train to make the journey to Washington, hoping to be present for the ceremony when the secretary of state issued his proclamation that the Nineteenth Amendment was part of the Constitution of the United States.

Joe Hanover was not with them. He had returned to Memphis to resume his law practice, and he would never again return to the General Assembly.

Not long after Catt's train had departed Nashville for the nation's capital, the Red Rose Brigade returned to Music City, summoned by Seth Walker.

Speaker Walker wired the secretary of state, emphatically stating, "Tennessee has not ratified the Nineteenth Amendment. This legislature has no power to act and has not acted."

He summoned the House back into session to run through a resolution nullifying the ratification of the amendment.

But it was too late for the Antis. By the time Walker himself took a train to Washington to deliver an alleged nullification resolution to Colby, the proclamation ceremony had concluded early on the morning of August 26, and the Nineteenth Amendment was officially in the Constitution.

Like Walker, Catt and her party did not arrive in Washington prior to the proclamation ceremony. Having taken a circuitous route to DC through Chattanooga, they arrived in Washington late on the morning of August 26, just a few hours after the ceremony.

But upon arriving in Washington and hearing the news that the "Susan B. Anthony Amendment" was now, at long last, a reality, Catt proceeded immediately to the White House, where she thanked President Woodrow Wilson for his support.

That evening, the National American Woman Suffrage Association held a celebration at Poli's Theatre in downtown Washington.

Two days later, at noon on Saturday, August 28, church and school bells rang and factory whistles blared in communities across the United States. The noisy celebration was carried out at Catt's request and coordinated by a national organization that would soon live up to its name, the League of Women Voters.

As the bells chimed and the whistles blew, millions of women across America looked forward to voting in the upcoming elections. Among these new voters was Eleanor Roosevelt in Hyde Park, New York, who would be voting that November for her husband, Franklin, who was the Democratic nominee for vice president of the United States.

And in Memphis, Tennessee, Esther Frost Hanover was finally going to exercise a precious constitutional right that her son had won for her.

Suffrage strategists included US Sen. Kenneth McKellar, state Sen. Ernest Haston, Sue Shelton White, Gov. A. H. Roberts, and state Rep. Joe Hanover.

Joe Hanover married Jeanette Kaplan Hanover on February 4, 1929. They enjoyed traveling together throughout the world and hosting elaborate dinner parties at their home in Memphis. And they particularly shared a love for raising, training, and racing thoroughbred horses.

15

Election Day 1920
. . . and Beyond

Joe and Jean Hanover were kindred spirits who enjoyed traveling together throughout the world.

O n November 2, 1920, Esther Frost Hanover left her home on Broad Avenue in Binghampton and walked to the Lester School. There she cast her votes for the US president and governor of Tennessee, as well as her senator, congressman, and state legislative representative. She did not get to vote for her son Joe. His name was not on the ballot.

Joe did not run for re-election to the Tennessee General Assembly and never ran for elective public office again.

Instead, Joe devoted the next sixty years to five loves.

The first and most important was Jeanette Kaplan Hanover, whom he married on February 4, 1929. Jean Hanover was a stunningly beautiful woman. Many said she bore a striking resemblance to the actress Carole Lombard.

Joe and Jean Hanover were kindred spirits. They enjoyed traveling together throughout the world and hosting elaborate dinner parties at their home in Memphis. They particularly shared a love for raising, training, and racing thoroughbred horses.

Joe's second love was the law. The immigrant who as a boy studied the Constitution of the United States and particularly the Bill of Rights, and as a young man attended night law school while holding two jobs, became a powerful lawyer. He and his younger brother David, whom Joe had helped put through law school, created a law firm that would become Hanover, Hanover, Jalenak, and Walsh, one of the most influential firms in Memphis and the state of Tennessee.

Despite the fact that Joe was not a "Crump lawyer," as he derisively referred to members of the Memphis Bar who were devoted to Boss Crump, powerful Memphis clients hired him because of his independence.

In 1938, Tennessee Gov. Gordon Browning appointed the highly respected lawyer Joe Hanover as the Shelby County district attorney. This outraged Joe's old nemesis, Boss Crump, whom Joe had often called a "tyrant."

When Joe went to the Shelby County Courthouse to be sworn in as district attorney, he found that no judge would administer him the oath of office. Boss Crump had instructed every judge in the courthouse to deny Joe the ceremony he needed to become DA.

Undaunted, Joe went to Nashville, where he found a judge who administered the oath.

Joe returned to Memphis to begin his work as district attorney only to find his new office empty. On orders from Boss Crump, all of the assistant DAs and the entire office staff had resigned. Crump had even dismissed the grand jury, leaving Joe the district attorney in title only.

A legal battle followed. It was one of the few that Joe lost in his career, so he returned to private law practice.

But Boss Crump's brief closing of the district attorney's office made Joe an even more powerful private attorney. He was in demand because of his independence and courageous advocacy for his clients.

Joe's third love was the Mississippi, the majestic river that had won his heart and imagination when he was a schoolboy sitting on the levee, admiring the traffic of steamboats and barges. He served as chairman of the Shelby County Port Commission and vice president of the Lower Mississippi Valley Flood Control Association, and he was a member of the National Rivers and Harbors Congressional Advisory Committee. In these positions, he led the

Mississippi River Commission in creating a twelve-foot-deep channel on the river from Cairo, Illinois, to New Orleans, making Memphis a major port in the South. For this and other work in improving river transportation to and from Memphis, the Memphis Civitan Club gave Joe the unofficial title "Old Man River," which absolutely delighted him.

His fourth love was the children of Memphis, particularly boys. While he and Jean had no children, Joe became a supporter of literally thousands of them. He was the president of Memphis Boys Town, and for forty-two consecutive years he paid for Christmas dinners for the boys at Gaither Hall, the Boys Town home. He was also a leader of Tall Trees, a transition institution for first-time juvenile offenders.

And then there were his horses. The Binghampton boy who loved watching horses race around the track at the Memphis Fairgrounds grew up to be a lawyer often seen with a law book in one hand and the *Daily Racing Form* and a cigar in the other.

Jean shared Joe's love of horses, and the two of them raised and trained thoroughbreds on a nine-acre farm near Germantown, Tennessee, in east Shelby County. They entered their horses in races at Oaklawn Track in Hot Springs, Arkansas, where they had a box. They also entered them in other races across the country, including the Preakness.

Joe and Jean named their thoroughbreds after prominent Memphis friends. Among their prized horses was a beautiful filly named Kem W. after Kemmons Wilson, the founder of Holiday Inn. Other horses were named Governor Ellington, after the Tennessee governor, and Bill Morris, after the Shelby County mayor and sheriff. Their stud was Riley, named after county trustee Riley Garner.

Joe's favorite horse was Mr. D. Thomas, named after Joe's friend Danny Thomas, the entertainer who founded St. Jude Children's Research Hospital. Mr. D. Thomas won the Arkansas Derby and, in Joe's words, "paid boxcars!"

Joe never named one of his horses Boss Crump, although he once commented that he might name a mule after Crump.

In all his pursuits, Joe never forgot why he waged war for woman suffrage in August 1920. While he was devoted to his wife, Jean, he was something of an incorrigible flirt. His family and friends recall many times over the years when

Joe would meet a young woman. He would ask her, "Do you vote?" When she responded, "Yes," Joe would laugh and say, "Well, you can thank me for that! I got you the right to vote!"

Mr. Joe, as he was known to his law partners and friends, died on April 4, 1984, at the age of ninety-five, nearly ninety years after crossing that frozen lake in Poland to find a new home in a land of opportunity and freedom.

He dearly loved his adopted country and its democratic ideals and had devoted much of his life to making those ideals a reality for every citizen.

Illustration by Wanda Stanfill based on Memphis Press-Scimitar photo
Joe and Jean Hanover named their thoroughbreds after
prominent Memphis friends. Their stud was Riley, named
after county trustee Riley Garner.

In later years, Joe Hanover served on several commissions affecting the development of the Mississippi River channel and Memphis as a major port. The Memphis Civitan Club named him 'Old Man River' for his efforts.

Epilogue: Joe Hanover Returns to Memphis

Joe Hanover and his law firm partners in Hanover, Hanover, and Walsh Law Firm. Eventually, the firm became Hanover, Walsh, Jalenak & Blair, PLLC. Then the firm merged with Harris, Shelton, Dunlap, Cobb & Ryder, PLLC, founded in 1956, to create Harris Shelton Hanover Walsh, PLLC.

early 100 years after he successfully led the fight for ratification of the Nineteenth Amendment in the Tennessee legislature, Joe Hanover would return to Memphis. Beginning in early 2020, he would proudly stand behind the University of Memphis Law School, facing his beloved Mississippi River.

He would not be alone. Standing alongside him would be his suffrage sisters, including crusader Ida B. Wells, Mary Church Terrell, Marion Griffin, Charl Ormond Williams, Lois DeBerry, Lide Smith Meriwether, Lulu Colyar Reese, Alma Law, Minerva Johnican, Maxine Smith, Frances Loring, and Happy Snowden Jones. Adjacent to the *Equality Trailblazers* monument is the state historical marker honoring an earlier Tennessee suffragist, Elizabeth Avery Meriwether of Memphis.

Joe and his suffrage sisters would not be present in flesh and blood. They would be in bronze, beautiful statues designed by Nashville artist Alan LeQuire, who had previously created sculptures recognizing Tennessee suffragists in Knoxville and Nashville. The steadfast Shelby County legislative delegation members who joined Joe in voting for the amendment are also mentioned on the monument: state senators Lambert E. Gwinn and Frank J. Rice along with representatives Ernest Bell, George A. Canale, Carl Larsen, C. E. McCalman, John Morgan, and T. K. Riddick.

Hanover and his sisters would stand at the Memphis portion of the Tennessee Woman Suffrage Heritage Trail, extending from one end of the Volunteer State to the other.

The trail enables Tennesseans and tourists to see Carrie Chapman Catt at Centennial Park in Nashville, Harry Burn at the Market Square in Knoxville, Sue Shelton White in front of City Hall in Jackson, and Joe Hanover and his Memphis sisters on a visit to the Mississippi riverfront.

A group gathered at Bounty on Broad, a trendy restaurant in Binghampton, to celebrate Joe's "homecoming." The crowd included Hanover family members with fond memories of "Uncle Joe"; partners from the old law firm of Hanover, Hanover, Jalenak, and Walsh; and even some modern-day suffragists such as Paula Casey and Jocelyn Wurzburg who led the campaign to build the *Equality Trailblazers Memphis Suffrage Monument* so the legacy of Joe and his sisters would never be forgotten and, in fact, is carried forward.

The restaurant was the perfect location to remember Joe and his incredible life. It is in the building that was Joe's first home in Binghampton, where W. C. Hanover & Sons was located on the ground floor with the Hanover home on the second floor.

The group convened on the second floor, dining at tables in the very room where young Joe had first read the Declaration of Independence and the Constitution of the United States of America.

They shared and admired photos of Joe and the new bronze statue of him that would soon grace the campus of his alma mater law school. His family reminded the attendees that President Woodrow Wilson called Joe the day after the vote to congratulate him.

They raised a toast in Joe's honor and also honored the courage of his father, Wolfe, and his mother, Esther, who brought Joe and his brothers to a new home of freedom and opportunity. It is ironic that Poland enfranchised women in 1918, two years before the United States did.

Then, in conversation, it was noted that a century after Joe had helped secure the ratification of the Nineteenth Amendment to the Constitution of the United States, there were still people and forces in America who were trying to deny people the right to vote or make it difficult for them to do so.

It was agreed that if Joe Hanover had been present, he would have reminded the group that democracy remained a work in progress and that there was still unfinished business.

J. HANOVER, owner "Jerelyn A." JOCKEY CLYDE BRAMBLE up
Miss A Win - 2nd   R. LAWSON, trainer
Indian Storm - 3rd   June 2, 1979
4 & 1/2 Furls. 54:1   Commodore Downs

J. Hanover, owner. Jerelyn A. Miss A Win, second, Indian Storm, third. Jockey Clyd Bramble up. R. Lawson, Trainer. June 2, 1979, Commodore Downs.

Photo courtesy of the Hanover family

River Downs. J & J Hanover owners, 'Bull Man,' L.L. Sackett, trainer. B. Sackett.

Illustration by Wanda Stanfill based on a Memphis Press-Scimitar photo
While Joe and Jean Hanover had no children, he was the president of
Memphis Boys Town, and for forty-two consecutive years, he paid for
Christmas dinners for the boys at Gaither Hall, the Boys Town home.

Bibliographic Essay

Prologue: The Lobby of The Hermitage Hotel, August 18, 1920

The iconic Hermitage Hotel in Nashville was indeed the "third house" of the Tennessee General Assembly in August 1920 and the eye of the storm in the "War of the Roses."

The descriptions of the lobby, anterooms, and suites of the hotel at that time are based on discussions with and information provided by The Hermitage Hotel's longtime director, Tom Vickstrom, and also on Ridley Willis II's wonderful book, *The Hermitage at One Hundred: Nashville's First Million-Dollar Hotel* (Providence House, 2009).

The chronology of the seventy-two-year-long battle for woman suffrage is found in Carol Lynn Yellin's "Countdown in Tennessee, 1920," *American Heritage*, December 1978; *The Perfect 36: Tennessee Delivers Woman Suffrage* (Vote 70, Inc., 1998) by Carol Lynn Yellin and Dr. Janann Sherman; and Elaine Weiss's *The Woman's Hour: The Great Fight to Win The Vote* (Viking, 2018).

The history of how the fight for woman suffrage came down to the Volunteer State in August 1920 is also based on "The Final Battle," by Paula F. Casey, *Tennessee Bar Journal*, September–October 1995, pp. 20–23.

Chapter 1—A Frozen Lake in Poland

The account of Joe Hanover and his family's remarkable journey to America is based on Carol Lynn Yellin and Dr. Janann Sherman's "The Man Who Took Democracy Seriously," in *The Perfect 36*, supra.

Chapter 2—A New Life . . . in Memphis and Binghampton

There are numerous sources for a narrative history of Memphis, among them, G. Wayne Dowdy's *A Brief History of Memphis* (The History Press, 2011); Preston Lauterbach's *Beale Street Dynasty: Sex, Song, and the Struggle for the Soul of Memphis* (Norton and Company, 2015); and *Metropolis of the American Nile* (Windsor Publications, 1982) by John E. Harkins.

The history of the Pinch District of downtown Memphis in the late nineteenth century is found on the Tennessee Encyclopedia website.

The description and history of Binghampton, including the Hanovers' home and business on Broad Avenue, are based on Vance Lauderdale's "A 1911 View of Broad Avenue in Memphis," *Memphis Magazine*, June 2015.

The photo of Broad in 1911 was provided by Lily Witham and published with her permission.

The story of the Hanover family's moves, first to the Pinch and then to Binghampton, was based on interviews with Joe's grandnephews Eddie Kaplan and Brad Hanover.

Chapter 3—Why Can't Mother Vote?

The account of the Hanover family's love for their new country, the United States of America, and the encouragement Joe and his brothers received from their parents to read the Constitution and the Declaration of Independence is found in Joe Hanover's reminiscences in "A Lost Man Found," *The Wheel* (Women's Resource Center of Memphis, November 1978). This includes Joe's memory of asking his parents why his mother could not vote.

The documentation of the naturalized citizenships of Wolfe and Esther Hanover was provided by Brad Hanover in correspondence from his father, J. Alan "Skippy" Hanover.

Chapter 4—A Calling to Law

Joe's memories of attending the Market Street School in downtown Memphis are found in "Hanover Wins Carley Award for Making River Work," Louis Silver, the *Commercial Appeal*, April 20, 1966.

The story of his attendance and graduation from night law school is found in "Joseph Hanover and the Fight for Woman's Suffrage," by Michael Kelly in *Memphis Bar Association Magazine*, December 1993. This includes the history of Hanover's law career, including the establishment with his brother David of the law firm that became Hanover, Hanover, Jalenak, and Walsh.

Chapter 5—The Election of an Independent

The story of Edward H. "Boss" Crump's domination of Memphis and

Tennessee politics for the first fifty years of the twentieth century can be found in numerous sources, among them, *Historic Memphis Biographies*; David Tucker's "Edward Hull Boss Crump," *Tennessee Encyclopedia*, 2017; and Otis Sanford's *From Boss Crump to King Willie* (University of Tennessee Press, 2017).

Joe's surprising election as an independent in 1918 in Boss Crump's Memphis was also recounted in Jo L. Potter's "A Different Kind of Race: Memphian Joe Hanover and the Passage of the Nineteenth Amendment," *Memphis Jewish Journal*, October 2003.

Shelby County election commissioner Robert Meyers and Carol Collinsworth, Shelby County election commissioner outreach specialist, also provided information regarding Joe Hanover's election to the Tennessee legislature.

Chapter 6—The Fight for Partial Suffrage

The story of the successful fight led by freshman legislator Joe Hanover in 1919 to win partial suffrage for Tennessee women is found in Carol Lynn Yellin and Dr. Janann Sherman's *The Perfect 36*.

Chapter 7—Removal and Re-election

This chapter is based on information provided by Ronald A. Lee, the assistant director for reference services at the Tennessee State Library and Archives, and the following news accounts:

- "Shelby Legislators Held Disqualified," the *Tennessean*, August 2, 1919, p. 3.
- "Memphis Lawyer in Race for Assembly," the *Tennessean*, July 27, 1920, p. 7.

Chapter 8—A Summons from Mrs. Catt

The primary sources for the account of Carrie Chapman Catt's call to Joe to assume the leadership of the fight for woman suffrage in the Tennessee House of Representatives are Carol Lynn Yellin's "Countdown in Tennessee," Carol Lynn Yellin and Dr. Janann Sherman's *The Perfect 36*, and Elaine Weiss's *The Woman's Hour*, supra.

Chapter 9—The Battle of the Women of Faith

The principal source for this chapter is Jean Roseman and her wonderful book, *Shalom Nashville*.

Chapter 10—"You're a Pretty Cheap Vote— They Are Paying Others a Thousand!"

The challenges that Joe faced as he fought for the ratification of the Nineteenth Amendment in the Tennessee House of Representatives are summarized in many accounts, including those of Carol Lynn Yellin, Dr. Janann Sherman, and Elaine Weiss, referenced above. But my primary sources for this chapter were the memories of Joe himself as set forth in two articles: "Memphian Pulled the Lever That Gave Vote to Women," Nancy Hart, *Memphis Press-Scimitar*, November 20, 1970, p. 8; and "Hanover Recalls His Fight for the Nation's Women," Rondell Beck, *Memphis Press-Scimitar*, June 25, 1979.

Chapter 11—"A White Man's Country!"

There are numerous news accounts of the final debate about woman suffrage between Speaker Seth Walker and Joe Hanover in the Tennessee House of Representatives on August 17, 1920. One of the most interesting and comprehensive was from a somewhat obscure source, the *Daily Gate City and Constitution* (Keokuk, Iowa). Its lead story on August 18, 1920, ("Tennessee House Delays Suffrage Vote") quotes in detail from the final speeches of Speaker Walker and Representative Hanover and describes the parliamentary moves that followed. It was the primary source for this chapter.

Chapter 12—"The Hour Has Come!"

The dramatic events of the vote on ratification of the Nineteenth Amendment are wonderfully described in the works of Carol Lynn Yellin, Dr. Janann Sherman, and Elaine Weiss, referenced above, and Joe's own recollection in news accounts, also referenced above.

Chapter 13—False Affidavits and the Red Rose Brigade Heads for Alabama

There were two primary sources for this chapter on the bizarre events that occurred in the aftermath of the Tennessee General Assembly ratifying the Nineteenth Amendment. The first was the account in the *Nashville Tennessean*, August 19, 1920, "Tennessee Ponders Rescission of Woman Suffrage Ratification." The other was Joe's recollection, particularly of the Red Rose Brigade, as set forth in "A Lost Man Found," *The Wheel*, supra.

Chapter 14–Signed, Sealed, and Delivered

The source for this chapter was "Liberty Bell" in Elaine Weiss's *The Woman's Hour*, supra.

Chapter 15–Election Day 1920 . . . and Beyond

The chapter on Joe's remarkable life after he left the Tennessee General Assembly in 1920 is based on interviews with his grandnephews Eddie Kaplan, Brad Hanover, and Jerry Schwartz, as well as his grandniece Phyllis Levine. It is also based on numerous news accounts, including "Mr. Joe at Age 91–I've Still Got a Lot to Do," Larry Williams, the *Commercial Appeal*, March 22, 1981; "Semi-Retired Lawyer's Castle Is Ranch-Style Home," Mary George Beggs, the *Commercial Appeal*, September 15, 1979; and "Services Today for Joseph Hanover, Suffrage Champion," the *Commercial Appeal*, April 5, 1984.

Epilogue–Joe Hanover Returns to Memphis

The story of the creation and dedication of the *Equality Trailblazers Memphis Suffrage Monument* is based upon conversations with Paula Casey, chair of the Memphis Suffrage Monument committee, and Alan LeQuire, who created the bust of Joe Hanover that is on the monument.

Joe Hanover and Sam Hanover walk down Broad Avenue in Memphis.

Index

A

Anshei Sphard, *18*
Anthony Amendment, *4-5, 98*
Anthony, Susan B., *4, 55, 64, 98*

B

Bloomstein, Elizabeth Lee, *62, 65*
Bounty on Broad, *112*
Burn, Harry, *84-86, 91-92, 112*
Bush, Paul, *3-4, 72*
Boys Town of Memphis, *105, 116*

C

Catt, Carrie Chapman, *6-7, 40, 52, 54-59, 64, 69, 71, 79, 86, 97-98, 112, 119*
Colby, Bainbridge, *97-98*
Constitution of the United States, *3-4, 6-7, 20, 22, 24, 28, 34-35, 42, 48, 56, 70, 76-77, 85, 97-98, 104, 112-113, 118*
Cox, James T., *84-85*
Crump, Edward H., *30, 33-35, 56-57, 104-105, 118-119*
Czar of Russia, *11, 17-18, 23-24, 30, 34*

D

DeBerry, Lois, *111*
Declaration of Independence, *20, 24, 28, 34-35, 112, 118*
Dudley, Anne Dallas, *55, 71*
Dudley, Guilford, *55*

G

Garner, Riley, *105, 107*

H

Handy, W. C., *33*

Hanover, Hanover, Jalenak, and Walsh, *104, 110, 112, 118*
Hanover, David, *ix, 18-19, 28-29, 104, 118*
Hanover, Esther, *10-13, 20, 22-24, 42, 98, 103, 112, 118*
Hanover, Jean, *100, 102-103, 105, 107, 116*
Hanover, Joseph
—Escape from Poland, *11-13, 35, 40, 117*
— Boyhood in Binghampton, *16-19, 23-24, 27-28, 117-118*
—Legal education, *28-29, 118*
—Law career, *28-29, 47, 104, 121*
—Election to legislature, *34-35, 118-119*
—Removal from legislature and re-election, *47-50, 119*
—Selection to lead the fight for ratification of the Nineteenth Amendment, *7, 52, 59, 119*
—Final debate, *7, 77-79, 120*
—Marriage to Jean Kaplan Hanover, *100, 103*
—Appointment as district attorney, *104*
—Love of thoroughbred horses, *18, 27, 100, 103, 105, 107*
—Chancellor of Boys Town, *105, 116*
—Return to Memphis, *97, 111-113*
Hermitage Hotel, The, *x, xiv, 2, 5-6, 8, 55-57, 72, 86-87, 97, 117*

J

"Jack Daniel's Suite," *7, 58, 69*
Johnican, Minerva, *111*

K

Kuhn, Agnes, *65*

L

Louisville and Nashville (L&N) Railroad, 6-7, 56
LeQuire. Alan, 111, 121
Lusky, Lettie, 65

M

Market Street School, 27-28, 118
McKellar, Sen. Kenneth, 6, 56, 99
Meriwether, Elizabeth Avery, 111
Mills, Helen Wile, 65
Mississippi and Shelby County Port Commission, 27, 104-105
Mississippi River, 12, 17, 27, 104-105, 108, 111-112
Morris, Bill, 105

N

Nineteenth Amendment, vii, xiv, 3, 5-6, 42, 48-50, 52, 56-59, 60, 63, 65, 70, 76-79, 84-87, 91, 94, 97-98, 111, 113, 119-121

O

Overton, Austin, 84

P

Partial suffrage, 4, 36, 40-42, 47-48, 55, 58, 78, 119
Pearson, Josephine, 6, 56-57, 63-65
Pinch District of Memory, 12, 16, 18, 27, 118
Pleasant, Gov. Ruffin, 48
Pogroms, 11, 17
Poland, 7, 34, 11-12, 18, 24, 34-35, 40, 76, 106, 112
Pollitzer, Anita, 58

R

Red Rose Brigade, 90, 93, 97, 121
Riddick, T. K., 59, 112

Roberts, Gov. A. H., 3, 5-6, 36, 41, 49, 56-58, 72, 84-85, 93-94, 97, 99
Ryman Auditorium, 7, 57, 91

S

Seneca Falls Meeting, 4
Smith, Maxine, 111
Southern Law School, 28
Suffrage Heritage Trail, 112

T

Teitlebaum, Sarah Lowenstein, 65
Tennessean, 92, 119, 121
Tennessee League of Women Voters, 57, 98
Terrell, Mary Church, 111
Thomas, Danny, 105
Thompson, Frank M., 48, 70
Turner, Banks, 84-85, 92

U

United States Supreme Court
—Decision in Minor v. Happersett, 4
University of Memphis Law School, 111
Upton, Harriet, 97

V

Vertrees, John, 42
Vertrees, Virginia, 42

W

W. C. Hanover & Sons, 16, 18-19, 28, 112
Walker, Seth, 6, 41-42, 56, 58-59, 69-70, 77-79, 83-86, 92-93, 97-98, 120
"War of the Roses," 3, 6, 57, 63, 83, 117
Wells, Ida B., 111
White, Sue Shelton, 58, 99, 112
Williams, Charl, 6, 90, 92, 97, 111
The Women's Bible, 64
Women's Christian Temperance Union, 7, 42, 56

About the Author

Bill Haltom lives and writes in Memphis and Monteagle, Tennessee. This is his eighth book.

For more information, visit www.billhaltom.com.